THE
METAPHYSICS
OF
Shoes

THE
METAPHYSICS
OF
shoes

12 Extraordinary Steps to
Empower Your Sole's Journey

CHARLINE E. MANUEL

BALBOA.
PRESS

A DIVISION OF HAY HOUSE

Library of Congress Control Number: 2012905481

Balboa Press books may be ordered through booksellers or by contacting:

Balboa Press
A Division of Hay House
1663 Liberty Drive
Bloomington, IN 47403
www.balboapress.com
1-(877) 407-4847

ISBN: 978-1-4525-4954-5 (e)
ISBN: 978-1-4525-4956-9 (sc)
ISBN: 978-1-4525-4955-2 (hc)

Printed in the United States of America

Balboa Press rev. date: 05/25/2012

*For Greg, who asked the question, and for all those
whose lives will be blessed by the answer.*

How beautiful are thy feet with shoes, O prince's daughter!
SONG OF SOLOMON 7:1

Contents

Acknowledgments xi

Introduction: *For the Love of Shoes*.................................xiii

1 *Baby Shoes*...1

2 *Dancing Shoes*...8

3 *A Man and His Gators*... 19

4 *Stilettos*.. 26

5 *Shoe Shine*... 33

6 *Footprints in the Snow*... 45

7 *In His Shoes*... 56

8 *Lucky Shoes*... 68

9 *Bloody Soles*... 76

10 *Broken Heel*.. 89

11 *Bowling Shoes*..101

12 *Royal Sandals*..114

In Summary 130

Conclusion..132

About the Author 136

Acknowledgments

Writing this book was a labor of love, and those who loved me through the process made my labor worthwhile.

I am grateful to the caring friends and family who did not even flinch when I told them I was writing an inspirational book using *shoes* as the theme.

My heart is filled with appreciation for my daughter, Tiffany, who believed with me that this book was indeed a good idea, and who also believed I could write it.

Thank you to Reverend Prentiss Davis, Wilma Moore Black and Ibrahim Ramey for the feedback and editorial assistance on the extremely rough first draft.

To my family and loved ones, whose life experiences inspired the stories in the book, I give a sincere thank-you for being in my life.

To "Billy," a big thank-you is appropriate. Who knew back in second grade that your instigations would become a motivation for my persistence to write what I hope is a number one best-selling book?

Last but not least, I am grateful for the publishing staff at Balboa Press for helping to bring this book into physical form.

Introduction

For the Love of Shoes

Shoes have been on my mind since I was in the second grade. Not directly, nor consistently, but as part of the thoughts, feelings, and emotions stored in the memory bank of my subconscious mind. It was when a male friend asked me a few years ago, "Why do women love shoes so much?" that I began to explore my "love" for shoes. I didn't have a clear answer to his question at the time. Back then, I thought my love for shoes was about the beauty, color, and style of the variety of shoes that just seemed to look good on my feet. *How beautiful are thy feet with shoes, O prince's daughter!* (Song of Solomon 7:1) For me, this scripture said it all.

However, my friend's question stayed with me. I thought about it until I came up with some clues from my past and made some revealing discoveries. I was able to pinpoint two early childhood experiences that have caused shoes to be on my mind for over fifty years now. Just as my friend suggested, I am guilty of being one of those women who love shoes and shopping for them. As I recalled some of the key stories from my life, I realized that my love went much deeper than simply enjoying the beauty of a good-looking pair on my feet. Now I can address my friend's question: Our love for shoes is not just about shoes. Behind our outer attention to them are life stories that involve experiences in places where our shoes have taken us, and the hope of where they will take us in the future. The stories from our pasts hold pain that challenged us to grow, as well as pleasures that caused us to celebrate. Either way, our shoes hold us up and carry us through the changing seasons of our lives. Future stories await the arrival of our shoes on the terrain of unfulfilled dreams, the road toward personal victory over life's circumstances, and the pathway to satisfy the divine compulsion to strive for our highest potential. For the shoe lover, shoes provide the opportunity to customize our journey with our own personal taste, style, and attitude, an opportunity to make our own unique set of footprints on that which we deem worthy of our time and attention. How we adorn our feet is more than a fashion statement; it announces a particular perspective of how we see ourselves going forward from wherever we are to wherever we want to go, to do whatever is before us to do. Yes, we love shoes, but we also seize the chance to dress our feet appropriately for our various levels of excitement, intention, and outlook while traveling on our unique expeditions through this lifetime.

The Metaphysics of Shoes provides an opportunity to delve into our own personal experiences and discover that we all have shoe stories. They're not unique to women, and each person's story is based on one's own "sole's" journey—where that person has been and where he or she hopes to go. This book is about the empowering lessons embedded in our real-life parables. Just like the narratives we live, the stories written herein reflect hope, love, and joy as well as fear, struggle, and challenge. In each story, there are also learning opportunities that can make a positive impact on our lives and those of others. Let me explain by sharing two stories from my childhood.

I am the seventh child of a family of eight children. I was born severely pigeon-toed, a condition that has both feet turning inward. Because it was difficult to walk, I had to wear doctor-prescribed corrective shoes. The process of going shoe shopping should have been dull since the only selection involved a choice between brown and black. However, the experience turned out to be a special time that made a deep and lasting mark on my life.

The few times I had my mother's full attention all to myself were when she took me for the prescription, fitting, and purchase of shoes. In the 1950s, the stores in Detroit that sold corrective shoes were located in out-of-the-way places and far from doctors' offices. It took my mother and me a half day of traveling by bus and at least two to three visits to complete the acquisition of a single pair of shoes. Since none of my brothers and sisters wanted so much as to be seen in a store that only had "boring" shoes, it was just Mom and me on our missions. So for me, acquiring a pair of shoes was an event, one that nurtured the development of a deep and lasting connection with my mother. On those days spent together, Mom and I talked about everything imaginable; it was our special time. We built a close relationship on those Saturdays sitting on the bus, with me asking many questions and Mom responding in her loving and wise way.

As mentioned, it was in the second grade that the joy of shopping for shoes expanded to a new level; the seeds for my love of shoes were planted in my heart and mind. My birthday is in December, so I was not allowed to start kindergarten until I was almost six. That meant I was a bit taller than many of my classmates. And I was chubby, so that's what they called me. I wore thick glasses with light blue frames. A silver chain dangled from them and wrapped around my neck—Mom's assurance that I wouldn't lose them. My clothes were worn and a bit too large on me since they were hand-me-downs from my older sister. I had long, thick hair that would not stay braided for the whole school day despite my mom's best efforts. And of course, I wore corrective shoes. To say I was awkward-looking is being kind. I accepted the teasing and learned to deal with it by putting my face in books and living in a fantasy world of my own.

When a boy (I'll call him Billy since I don't remember his real name) teased me in second grade, something changed in me. As best I can remember on that life-changing day, the scene went something like this: "Look at her," Billy said to a group of children standing in the hallway as I approached. "She's so ugly . . . and look at her baby shoes." The children around him seemed to agree and began laughing and pointing at my shoes. Then the worst happened. As Billy chanted "baby shoes, baby shoes, baby shoes," the other children joined in. A teacher came to my rescue after a few horrible minutes, but the damage had been done. I was hurt, not just because they were teasing me—I was used to that—but up until that time, no one had ever made a big deal about my corrective shoes. I felt the words "baby shoes" piercing my body. It especially hurt because I had a crush on Billy, and up until that experience, I thought he had a crush on me too. On top of being publicly humiliated, I had my first heartbreak.

To make matters worse, Mom had me wear corrective shoes year-round until I was nearly eleven, long after the doctor stopped prescribing them for me. In all fairness, Mom wanted to be sure my feet were perfect so she "sentenced" me to a few extra years of wearing what was stuck in my mind as "baby shoes." However, it turned out that the teasing I received from Billy was just the beginning. The older I got, the more my "baby shoes" became a target for kids who needed someone to tease.

It should have been no surprise that when I got my first part-time job at sixteen and received my first paycheck, I bought two pairs of shoes. With the newfound freedom of having my own money and not having to wear corrective shoes, I was officially a shoe lover, and I had the added distinction of loving to shop for them as well.

Over the years, shopping for shoes became a kind of therapy for me. When I was feeling a little down, a trip to the shoe store would suddenly have me feeling better. The uplifting "therapy session" brought forth a resurgence of joy, comfort, and hope. When I could afford it (and sometimes when I couldn't), the purchase of cute shoes was my defense against Billy's indictment, allowing the awkward-looking second grader within me the chance to redeem herself as beautiful and worthy of love.

I have lived most of my adult life thinking my love for shoes was about them. And why not? Shoes in and of themselves have a lot to offer. When I shop, I love looking at them, touching them, trying them on, and admiring them on my feet. I enjoy giving my opinion if another shopper asks, "How do you think these look on me?" When I find a pair I truly like, I purchase it in several different colors. I enjoy inspecting the new styles and designs. I love planning an outfit around a new pair of shoes. But even with all this love, there is more to it.

As I began to examine the experiences that have shaped my relationship with shoes, I developed a curiosity about the experiences of others. Observing and listening to their stories, I became convinced that there are lessons we can learn from them. And we can use those lessons to grow in positive and inspiring ways.

For example, some of us will purchase and wear shoes that are too small, too tight, or too big. We seem generally uninterested or unaware of the fact that ill-fitting shoes can cause sore feet, bunions, calluses, cramped legs, lower back pain, and achy knees, for men and women alike. Part of this willingness to bear such pain is due to the change in the way we purchase shoes. Back in the 1950s, shoe stores had salespersons, or specialists. They would measure your feet first to determine an accurate size. They would put the shoes on your foot and then test to see if they were a good fit. A good specialist would be relentless in getting a good fit, even if it meant bringing out several different pairs of shoes. As time eliminated the personal touch, comfort fell by the wayside and we focused more on style, design, color, and so forth. So is any of this about a love for shoes? Yes and no.

Long ago, our ancestors discovered that feet demand protection in order to journey in hot and cold climates or to travel over rough and rocky roads. Shoes represent the armor and shield protecting us as we move forward on life's sometimes challenging pathways. What we've learned is that the quality of our footwear can support, delay, or even end our journey abruptly. When they're adequate for the path we're traveling, they add vitality to the steps we take and support our desire to go where we want to go. Shoes matter!

I had this awareness confirmed one day as I was observing one of my grandsons. Caleb, eighteen months old at the time, was attempting to get his father's attention. My son-in-law was busy at work on the computer and not responding to several cries of "Daddy!" So my grandson walked to the area next to the front door where the shoes of all the family members were perfectly lined up. He stood in front of the three smallest pairs: black tie-up shoes he wore to church on Sundays, sandals for when he rode in his stroller, and sneakers for when he rode his tricycle. Little Caleb stood looking at his three options for a moment and then picked up the sneakers. He carried them to where his father was working and just stood there holding the shoes until his father finally looked up and acknowledged him. My grandson had used his shoes to accomplish what his words had not been able to. At such an early age, he had already figured out that shoes are about going places, and he used them to communicate where he wanted to go and what he wanted to do.

The Metaphysics of Shoes includes twelve stories presented as a catalyst for contemplation, discussion, and self-discovery. Eleven were inspired by real-life themes from my own experiences or those of others. Some of the stories deal with emotionally charged subjects, yet I encourage you to stay with them until the end. Sometimes our greatest life lessons can emerge from experiences that cause us to transform pain to possibility. The idea for the twelfth story was inspired by a parable found in the Holy Bible. Its timeless message describes the most important journey our shoes will carry us on: the journey of love, forgiveness, and reconciliation. At the end of each story is a short vignette, "Sole Thoughts," that offers a look into the deeper meaning and one possible life-lesson from the story. I say "one possible" because it is my hope that as you read, you will recall your own stories and thereby uncover your personal meanings. Next is "Extraordinary Step to Empower Your Sole's Journey," a short statement of how to implement the life-lesson going forward. At the close of each chapter, you will also find a list of probing questions under the heading "If the Shoe Fits." They're designed to stimulate your own self-discovery process. You can answer them by journaling or discussing them in a group. With your revelations, perhaps you will direct your own shoes toward new and wonderful pathways, courageously taking extraordinary steps toward your goals, dreams, and desires.

I use the word "metaphysics" in the title of the book with the realization that some metaphysicians may take issue with such a deep philosophy being applied to shoes. After all, it's a philosophy that deals in the realm of ideas, thoughts and the mind, and shoes deal with feet—two opposite spectrums of the body. I state my case by saying that everything has an existence in the invisible realm of ideas before manifesting in our visible world. Since metaphysics looks at the underlying meaning behind physical matter, so it is that behind every act of putting on a pair of shoes (or taking them off) is an idea that may hold a deeper belief, desire, and intention. As you will see in this book, the possibilities held in the thoughts, dreams, desires, and intentions behind a single pair of shoes are endless. When we look behind the stories of our lives, we find deeper messages, a metaphysical view, but more importantly, we find life-empowering ideals.

No matter what kind of shoes we wear, and how good they look on our feet, this may be the most important question: "Where are your shoes taking you?" They go where we direct them. And this is where the metaphysicians will agree: We map out the path that our shoes travel with what we think, believe, intend, feel, desire, and put our mental energy into.

So what's on your mind regarding where you want to go? Have you given your shoes the charge of supporting your walk into greater opportunities for love, wisdom, and prosperity? Have you harnessed the inner strength to outwardly strap on your marching boots and courageously proceed toward your passion, your purpose, your dreams? Are you clear about the beliefs you hold, causing you to stand tall in your shoes and claim the life you desire?

I have grown beyond my false childhood belief that the Billys of the world would like me, notice me, and respect me if I wore cute shoes. I still enjoy wearing cute shoes, and if a "Billy" likes them, great. But if a "Billy" doesn't like them, it's still great! Nowadays, my preferences are for my well-being, style, beauty, and comfort. Becoming aware of my shoe stories helped me realize that inner beauty, positive self-esteem, and feeling worthy of love can make an ordinary pair of shoes look fabulous.

May the stories here add strength and power to your walk into the many blessed and prosperous days before you.

It's time to put on your shoes and step into an empowering journey of self-discovery.

Charline. E. Manuel

Baby Shoes

IT HAD BEEN COLD THAT day. She'd taken extra care to bundle up her one-year-old baby girl for the long bus ride downtown. She had walked the three long blocks to the bus stop many times, but on that day, it seemed farther than usual. It was the same journey she had made on her way to the babysitter, both her jobs, and the grocery store. But she'd worked overtime the night before and slept only a few hours. Overtime meant a few more dollars to help make ends meet, so she worked the extra hours whenever possible. For a brief moment, she thought about turning around, but then she remembered that she had waited three weeks to get a Saturday appointment. So she did what she always did. Just around the time she reached the end of the second block, she held her baby girl a little tighter, adjusted the diaper bag on her shoulder, and moved her purse to the other hand. For the third time that day, she stopped to make sure the little brown paper bag she carried was neatly secured in the diaper bag. Each time she checked, it was there, safe.

When she arrived at the photography studio, there were several parents and children already waiting. She looked at the faces of the other parents and could see in their eyes that they wondered how old she was. She had seen that look many times in the past year. *I should just shout it out,* she thought. *I'm eighteen, and yes, this is my baby—and no, I'm not married!* Instead, she made her way to the last vacant seat in the waiting area, trying hard to avoid the stares she wanted so much to believe didn't matter to her.

She prepared herself for the long wait, which she didn't mind. It gave her an opportunity to warm up from the long journey. Her baby girl had fallen asleep on the bus ride and seemed heavier to carry. Nevertheless, the baby's limp body made it easier to maneuver the diaper bag, purse, gloves, hat, and the heavy clothing required for winter days in Michigan. She took great care not to wake the sleeping angel on her shoulder as she waited patiently like all the other parents.

Finally, when she was called, she leaped to her feet. The sudden move caused her daughter to open her brown eyes and begin looking around with curiosity. She planted a soft kiss on the girl's forehead, which seemed to assure the child that she was safe.

"Please come this way, miss," the saleswoman said. She led the young mother to a small bright yellow room with lots of pictures on the wall. The saleswoman placed a large folder on the table. "You may begin looking at these. I'll be back in a few minutes to take your selections."

When the young mother saw the first picture in the stack, a huge smile stretched across her face. She nodded, admitting to herself that she had been right—her baby girl was indeed the most beautiful baby in the whole world. It was a tough decision selecting only one picture from the many beautiful poses, but one seemed to capture the essence of her little angel a little more than the others did.

The saleswoman returned. "Have you made your selections?"

"I'll take this one."

"Just one? Out of all these beautiful pictures? The cost decreases per picture the more you buy," she said as she looked through the selections. "Surely you want some for family and friends."

"Just this one," the proud mother said as she stared at the picture for a moment. "Yes, this is the one."

"Oh, I see," the saleswoman said as she began to place the others back in the folder. "Do you have the shoes?"

"Yes, I do." She reached into the diaper bag and pulled out the little brown paper bag she had been guarding with her heart. She removed a tiny pair of shoes as if she were handling a precious gift. "I tried to clean them up," she said as she handed them to the woman, "but they're still a little scuffed."

"Oh, don't worry about that. When we apply the bronze, you'll hardly notice it. A few scuff marks will add a bit of character to the whole thing. Shoes are made to be worn."

"It's hard to believe she wore them out so quickly." The young mother stared at the shoes, knowing it was the last time she would see them in their natural state. "She started walking early, at seven months. Even the doctor admitted that's early."

"Well, think of it this way," the saleswoman said. "She's got places to go, and she's not wasting any time."

Both women laughed.

"Adding the bronze will take about a week or so, and we can mail them to you so you don't have to come pick them up."

"That would be great. It's quite a long bus ride to get here, and the service is slow on Saturdays."

The young mother watched the saleswoman finish the paperwork and then place the tiny shoes in a plastic bag.

"With your deposit, your balance is nine dollars. That includes the picture, the bronzing of the shoes, the frame, and of course the shipping," the saleswoman said.

The young mother shifted her baby from one arm to the other so she could reach into her purse. She pulled out a tiny coin holder that held two five-dollar bills folded and stuffed in with the two quarters she would need for the bus ride home. She proudly handed the two wrinkled bills to the saleswoman. As she waited for her change, she began preparing her daughter for the long trip home.

"Here's your change and receipt." The saleswoman took another look at the little girl, who had watched quietly during the whole transaction. "She is such a good baby. Usually the ones we see are fussy and cranky from the long wait." She touched the little girl's hand. "You are such a little blessing. You are a special baby."

"Yes, she is," the young mother said with great pride.

And then, in a moment, the thoughts of the past faded, and the young mother was a middle-aged woman again. Working two jobs for many years had been unkind to her body, but she had no regrets. She stood in the living room of her modest home, staring at the picture of her grown daughter draped in her cap and gown. Despite all she had gone through, to arrive at this moment was more than worthwhile. As she removed the old baby picture from the frame, she replaced it with the photograph of the adult version of her only daughter. She spoke to her as though she were present: "My daughter, the first in our family to receive a doctorate degree. My, oh my, how proud your grandmother would have been had she lived to see the woman you've become. What she dreamed for me has been fulfilled in you."

It had been twenty-nine years since she'd purchased the picture frame, yet the bronzed shoes looked new. Over the years, she had polished them as if idolizing her daughter's first steps, while at the same time adding strength to her current steps. She continued to talk to the young woman in the photo. "All these years, I hoped, I prayed, and God gave us both a strength we didn't know we had."

In that moment, she remembered interrupting her daughter's playtime when she was just eight years old: "What do you want to be when you grow up?" she had asked.

"I'm not sure. I haven't decided yet," the little girl said.

"Well, do you have any ideas?" the mother persisted.

"I can be anything I want to be," the little girl replied, and without another thought to the conversation, she returned to her playtime.

The mother stared at the picture for a long time, admiring the girl she had raised mostly on her own. She recalled the words of the saleswoman from so long ago: "She's got places to go, and she's not wasting any time." Just before she returned the frame to the mantel over the fireplace, she kissed her daughter's photograph, and then she kissed the shiny, bronzed shoes.

Sole Thoughts

A man's heart plans his way, but the LORD directs his steps.
PROVERBS 16:9

The successes we accomplish in life are set in motion by the mental and spiritual strength we harness to take the first step toward achieving them. The task of intentionally putting one foot in front of the other activates an inner power we don't know we have until it's used, a power our Creator built into our spiritual fabric. We decide what we want to achieve, for "a man's heart plans his way." One step at a time, the invisible hand of God guides us along the path, and the spirit of God not only divinely supports us but directs our steps as well. With each one, we grow into being what we must be in order to realize what we're working so diligently to achieve.

One example where we can see the unveiling of inner strength is in watching a child learn to walk. The child is willing to fall as many times as necessary just to take that first solid step. A baby's first pair of shoes marks the beginning of new possibilities for his or her life's journey. The first steps signal a major accomplishment, a child's first real success, perhaps a miraculous moment for the child. The small steps taken in those early months of life become building blocks of persistence and determination toward adulthood.

Children live in the bliss of pure possibility. This is one reason why it's said that they have great imagination. In those first hours, days, weeks, months, perhaps years, children instinctively feel destined for great things and a high-quality life. If we listen to the response of a child to the question "What do you want to be when you grow up?" we'll hear unbridled possibilities and untapped potential. As the years unfold, children are exposed to a conditioning process that robs them of the sweet innocence that drives the vivid, creative mind toward true potential. They find themselves forced to conform to the predominant thoughts, words, and actions of those around them. While some may be inspiring and positive, others may be negative and critical. The more children's dreams are discounted as pure fantasy, the further away they find themselves from being able to declare, "I can be anything I want to be." Their hopes are in danger of being squashed under the shoes of those who are not conscious of the importance of their steps, words, thoughts, and actions.

One of the greatest lessons that any adult can be mindful of is that we too were once children. Our own childhoods held important keys and insights into how we live our adult lives. We learned a lot about survival and growth in our formative years. Whether the path was smooth and easy or difficult and tough, we made it through. It was as children that we had our first glimpses of the hopes and dreams that propelled us forward in life. It was as children that we experienced disappointments that helped us discover our inner strengths. We face adult issues knowing we all survived childhood.

While some of our hopes and dreams fell by the wayside, others may still be dormant in the recesses of our minds. We may have abandoned some of our dreams out of ignorance of our own ability to persevere, or we may have traded them for something requiring a little less effort and strength. And yes, some of our dreams we actually achieved. Through it all, perhaps no one bronzed our baby shoes, but our first steps were the foundation that helped get us to where we are today.

In our story, a young mother saw her daughter's first steps as setting the tone of forward movement toward a destination that may have looked impossible many times along the way. As a teenage mother, she demonstrated the systematic principle of one step at a time. Day after day, year after year, she had the determination to work two jobs and harness the inner strength required to demonstrate what she had been praying for and working diligently to accomplish. She used the power of persistent movement to invest in the potential of her daughter, and the reward was one of grand success. In the story, we see a young mother set an example of hope and perseverance from which her child was able to capture and discover her own God-given gift of internal strength.

If there is a goal you want to achieve, take a solid step toward it, even if it's a baby step. Then take another. Know that with each move, you are building the idea of success in your mind. One step will lead to another, and another, and on and on. Your job is to keep moving. Before long, you'll realize that you're sprinting toward your goal and celebrating the inner strength it took to achieve it.

Extraordinary Step to Empower Your Sole's Journey

Harness your inner strength to take the first step toward some goal you want to achieve. Keep moving forward knowing that each step is being divinely directed.

If the Shoe Fits . . .

- Describe an experience where you used your personal inner strength to achieve a major goal.
- If your first pair of shoes had been bronzed, what value would that have for you today?
- Can you recall a goal that you achieved by using the "baby steps" method?
- Describe how you access the inner mental and spiritual strength that allows you to persevere through life's opportunities and challenges.
- What would be an Extraordinary Step toward drawing forth increased inner *strength* at this time in your life?

2

Dancing Shoes

THE JUDGE WAS TALKING. HIS lips were moving, but the young woman sitting at the defendant's table only pretended to be listening. Her thoughts were on the past, and the only thing she was hearing was the self-interrogation going on in her head: *What went wrong? What did I do that drove him away? Why is this happening to me?* The inner voice seemed to get louder and louder with each question. *So this is it? Did he ever really love me? How did we end up in divorce court? This whole thing makes no sense. Sure, we had a few problems; all couples have them. But divorce? Divorce?*

The sound of the judge's gavel brought Nancy's attention back to the moment, back to what felt like a bad dream. "Divorce granted," he said.

Her attorney turned and said, "Well, that's it, Nancy. You're a free woman."

Nancy had no words to speak, but her thoughts started up again: *But I don't want to be free. I want to be married. I want to go home with the man I thought was my soul mate. I want to stop at our favorite restaurant on the way home and have dinner with him, even if we eat in silence the way we have for the last two years.*

Nancy looked over at the plaintiff's table. John was already out of the courtroom. *He's going to be with her. Couldn't he just take a moment to say good-bye? Our marriage just ended, and he all but ran out of the courtroom.*

"Good luck," her attorney said as she extended her hand.

Nancy reached to shake the hand in front of her in what felt like slow motion. She knew it would be appropriate to speak, but the words would not come out. The voice in her head continued: *Good luck? What does that mean? My life just fell apart. What is this woman talking about? The only luck I want is to wake up and find that this whole thing has been a bad dream. John never had an affair, and I never caught him in lie after lie until he couldn't lie anymore.*

The attorney started talking again. "Nancy, if you don't mind a word of advice from someone who survived divorce, find a hobby quickly and start dating as soon as possible. Get back out there. The longer you wait, the harder it will be. I met my husband three weeks after I divorced my first husband, and now I'm happily remarried. There are some nice guys out there. You just have to look . . . and stay open." She turned to walk away and then stopped. "Oh, you'll get my final bill in a few days. I'd appreciate your attention to it as soon as you receive it. Business, you know." She walked away to meet her next client, a man who was waiting near the door. She shook his hand and led him into the hallway.

When Nancy walked into her house that evening, she sat on the sofa and the tears started to flow. Hours later, it was dark outside and dark in the house, and Nancy hadn't moved from her spot. The phone rang to interrupt her private pity party. She did not recognize the caller's phone number but decided to answer anyway. She cleared her throat in the hope that whoever was calling would not hear the sadness in her voice or suspect that she had been crying and sitting in the dark for hours.

"Hello."

"Hey, it's me." *John.* "I need to get the rest of my stuff out of the house. Can I come by tomorrow?"

How dare he call me on the night of our divorce? Why isn't he somewhere crying like me?

"Nanc? Are you there?" he asked.

"Yeah, sure, but please come by while I'm at work."

For what seemed like an eternity, there was dead silence on the line.

"Nanc, I'm so sorry." John spoke in a caring voice, the way he had up until two years ago. His tone was remorseful, and his words should have been soothing, but to Nancy they were painful. "I just think this . . ."

Nancy interrupted. "Like I said, come tomorrow while I'm at work."

"Okay." John paused, seeming to wait to see if Nancy had anything else to say. She did not. "Well . . . I guess . . . that's it. I'll leave the key under the mat." He paused again; this time the silence was longer. "Take care of yourself. I mean it, Nanc."

"Good-bye, John."

As she hung up the phone, she started to cry again. *I can't believe he called me Nanc. Doesn't he know that when you divorce someone, you can't continue to call her by the name you gave her on your second date?* She'd held back the tears while she was on the phone so he wouldn't know that she planned to spend the rest of the night—maybe the next week, or even a few months—bawling like a baby. She didn't want him to know that her only plan of survival was to feel sad, alone, and rejected for as long as it took to recollect herself. She didn't want him to know that she had absolutely no idea how she was going to move on without him.

Her thoughts turned to anger. *How dare that attorney tell me to get a hobby! John was my hobby. He was my hobby for eight years. Before I met him, I danced. Dancing was my hobby. I danced four, sometimes five, days a week. I was planning to open my own dance studio. Jazz, ballet, tap—I did it all. And then he came into my life and changed everything. Everything changed. "Nanc," he said, "if you get a regular job, we can buy our dream house much faster and start a family." He didn't tell me I would someday be living alone in "our" dream home, without him, without any babies. Where is the family he promised me? Where is the little girl I see in my dreams? I did what he asked and took an office job so I could bring in more money. I gave up dancing so I could be a "good" wife, and I hoped that one day I would be a "good" mother. But here I am, alone. What am I supposed to do now?*

Nancy wallowed in her own tears and self-pity for several weeks. Every morning when she opened her eyes, the tears started. Some days she hollered. Some days she shouted. Some days she whimpered like a wounded kitten. But the tears flowed generously every day before work. When she came home each night, she turned the key in the front door, and the tears would start. She opened the door to find he wasn't sitting on the sofa watching TV. He wasn't asking her, "What's for dinner, babe?" He didn't yell to her, "Hey, since you're in the kitchen, bring me a beer." All the things she remembered caused the tears to flow, even those things she had complained about.

When she received the attorney's bill, there was a little note inside: "Dear Nancy, hope you are taking my advice. Remember, get a hobby and get back out there." The final bill was for seven hundred dollars. Nancy wondered if the advice was included in the price.

So what am I supposed to do? Pull out my old dancing shoes and start dancing again? First it was a cynical thought, but then she said it aloud. She liked hearing the sound of her voice absent of crying, screaming, or yelling. *I dreamed of being a dancer since I was a little girl. When I danced, I felt strong, alive, confident. And I was pretty good at it.* She went to the mirror in the bathroom and looked at the sad face staring back. She raised her voice in confrontation: "You can't spend the rest of your life in this pitiful existence of shame and disappointment. You heard your attorney. God knows you paid her enough money. Get on with it, Nancy! What's stopping you? Start dancing again. Do it! Do it! Do you want to live the rest of your life buried in self-pity? What's it going to be?"

The next day, Nancy woke up with dancing on her mind. It was the first morning in nearly a month that she woke up without crying a river of tears. Something within had shifted. She decided not to go into the office—and although she didn't have a real plan, she knew exactly where she wanted to go instead.

"May I help you?" asked a slender woman wearing a black leotard with a green wraparound skirt covering the lower half of her body.

"Hi, I've seen this place for years and wanted to stop in and see what kind of classes you offer," Nancy said.

"Glad you came in." The woman extended her hand. "I'm Jackie, the owner."

"I'm Nancy."

"Well, Nancy, we have classes for adults and children. Are you interested in dance for your daughter or—"

"No, it would be for me. I don't have any children. It's just that I used to be a dancer . . . years ago. I started dancing when I was four. I did tap, ballet, jazz, and some hip-hop. I even competed in high school and college. But that was, well . . . I haven't danced in eight years, so I thought I'd take some classes just to get back into it. Like a hobby."

"Sounds like you might be a better instructor than a student."

"I'm just looking for a hobby," Nancy said. "Someone recently told me to get one."

"Well, right now for adults I have jazz classes on Wednesdays and modern dance on Thursdays. Both are pretty popular classes. I have a large group of women who, like you, want to dance as a hobby. Most of them see dancing as a good way to get some exercise and a positive way to nurture themselves."

"That sounds exactly like what I'm looking for. When can I start?"

"Come this week. The classes are ongoing, so you can join anytime. With your dancing background, you'll catch on quickly to the routines. However, I must tell you that I'm going to sell the studio. I'm looking for a buyer now."

"Why? I mean . . . if you don't mind sharing. Why are you selling this beautiful studio? I see lots of cars parked here at least four or five days a week."

"Oh, it's not money related," Jackie said. "The studio provides me with a good income. I've put my heart and soul into building this business. Dancing is my dream. Like you, I've been dancing since I was a little girl. My mother bought me my first pair of dancing shoes when I was six. I'm selling because I'm getting married and moving to North Carolina."

"Oh . . . congratulations." Nancy wanted to sound positive about marriage, but her wounds were still too fresh. "I hope it lasts. I mean, I hope it works out." Nancy stumbled over her words. "I mean, I hope you'll be very happy married."

"Listen, Nancy, I don't know what your situation is, but . . . would you have any interest in buying the studio?"

"Me? No. I'm . . . I . . . ," Nancy stuttered. "See, I just got a divorce, and I'm only looking for a hobby so I can move on with my life. Dancing was my life before I got married, so I thought I might dance again, and then I can stop going home every night . . ." She stopped as tears started to form. Nancy batted her eyes a few times in hopes of avoiding an all-out waterfall.

"Oh, I'm so sorry." Jackie stepped to the counter, pulled a box of tissue from below, and handed it to Nancy.

"No, I'm the one who's sorry. I'm so embarrassed that all this is coming out like this. Up until now, I've been able to do my crying in private." She wiped her eyes with the first tissue and then blew her nose with the next. "It's just been so hard to even think of moving on. Dancing is the only thing that I ever truly loved to do. I'm just looking for some way to pull myself out of this dark hole of sadness I've fallen into."

"Come." Jackie took Nancy's arm. "I have a teapot in my office in the back. I'll make two cups of mango-peach."

"Please . . . I don't want to be any trouble," Nancy said.

"No trouble at all. I usually take a tea break this time of day anyway—and I don't have a class until much later."

Jackie poured tea into the bright red mugs that read DANCE, DREAM, DANCE. The women sat for three hours talking, Nancy mostly pouring out her pain and Jackie mostly listening. It was as if the two women were old friends. They shared. They laughed. They cried.

"So . . . how much are you asking for the studio?" Nancy asked.

"Well, I own the building, so the price includes the building and the business."

"Sounds expensive," Nancy said.

"Not really. The building is valued at sixty-five thousand dollars, and my accountant tells me the business is valued at about eighty-five thousand. I sponsor two annual youth dance competitions that do very well financially. Those competitions have been well attended over the last five years, and they have gained a good reputation for the studio. The youth classes are the bread and butter of the business. I've even received some grants from the local Council of the Arts Commission for the past few years. My overhead is low, and I teach most of the classes myself. Nancy, there are so many opportunities here for someone who loves dancing."

"A hundred and fifty thousand dollars?

"Yeah," Jackie said, "but there's wiggle room in those numbers. Since I don't need the money all at once, we could work out a payment schedule or something. I would love it if you bought this studio. I'd really like to leave here knowing my work for the last twelve years will go to someone who values dancing as much as you and I do. You'd be great for the studio, and the studio would be great for you."

"My expensive attorney did get a good settlement from my divorce. John didn't even fight it—guilt money, I think. If anything can pull me out of this misery, it's dancing."

"Imagine how good you'll feel taking something as painful as a divorce and turning it into an opportunity to live your dream."

"I never thought about it that way," Nancy said.

Jackie leaned toward Nancy and took her hand. "Nancy, you're a dancer. You have the gift of creativity. Use your gift to imagine a new life for yourself."

"You're right. You are so right. I've forgotten who I am and what I love to do. I'm a dancer, and I used to be good at it."

Jackie extended her hand, and both women gave a firm handshake. They stood up from the small table where they had been seated for hours and celebrated with a long hug.

"Thank you so much," Nancy said. "I'm alive again. I can feel it."

"No, thank you! Six months ago, I started visualizing the perfect buyer for the studio, and when you walked through the door, I just knew you were the answer to my prayer. There was something about you that . . . Well, I just knew. Now I can leave my studio with ease, knowing it's in good hands."

Nancy rushed home. This time when she turned the key, there was no trace of sadness. When she opened the door, she didn't even notice that John wasn't sitting on the sofa watching TV. She headed straight for her bedroom. She opened the door to her huge walk-in closet and stood looking around for a moment.

Where are they? I know they're here somewhere.

She looked at a series of boxes on the top shelf.

That has to be them!

She ran to the storage room, pulled out a three-tier step stool, and carried it back to the closet. Standing on the stool, she reached up until she could touch the lower of the three boxes. All three fell to the floor at once.

Yes! I knew I still had them.

She moved the step stool from the closet and sat cross-legged on the floor. She opened the first box and gasped. She removed a pair of black shoes that had been neatly wrapped in a pink velvet cloth before they were placed inside. She turned them over and ran her fingers over the taps on the bottom. Then she opened the second box and removed a beautiful pair of white ballet shoes that were wrapped in red silk cloth. She kissed the soft white satin tops of both shoes before placing them on top of their covering. Finally, she opened the third box. From inside a green satin cloth, she pulled out a pair of black lace-up shoes that were adorned with red and white beads. Remembering that she had worn them at her last hip-hop dance performance at the Jefferson Performing Arts Center, she laughed aloud. "I bought a dance studio," she said. She liked the sound of what she heard, so she repeated the words a second time but a little louder. "I bought a dance studio!"

Sole Thoughts

Weeping may endure for a night, but joy comes in the morning.
You have turned for me my mourning into dancing . . .
PSALM 30:5, 11

There are times in our lives when things don't go as we had hoped or planned. Whether the change we experience is by way of divorce, the end of a once-cherished friendship, the death of a loved one, the loss of a job, or a failed business, there are times when endings can be deeply painful. At times like these, it is natural to revert to one of the first responses to hurt that we learned—crying. What may be problematic is that while it's acceptable for babies and little children, generally we've been conditioned to believe that adults should avoid, hide, or limit our tears. However, if we are to heal from our disappointments and reclaim our ability to imagine the fulfillment of our dreams, it may be helpful to shed a few restorative tears. Our weeping can be a significant catalyst to our healing, if we do it right.

Tears can be therapeutic. The journey back from tough times begins with a good mental and emotional cleansing, and our tears may facilitate the process. It's important to let go of the pain we find ourselves engulfed in so that we can move forward with a fresh perspective. Without some form of release, we may carry our hurt and pain with us into the next experience, thereby tainting the outcome of what could otherwise be a great new beginning. Crying is a natural human response to life's difficult experiences. We did it the day we were born. The sound of our crying was the first time we heard our own voice. No one had to teach us how to cry; we just knew and began doing it moments out of the womb. What we have learned since then is that tears flow when we're extremely happy as well as when we face tough situations. Either way, crying is not good or bad—it's simply one way of expressing what's in our hearts and minds.

All too often, crying is considered a sign of weakness. However, our tears can help us empty our sorrows before we become containers for long-term pain and suffering. Crying can be a positive channel for healing.

Weeping is the state of crying in response to deep emotional pain. This form of emotional cleansing is usually associated with grief and mourning. It turns on the tear-duct faucet full blast, no withholding at all. This may involve wailing, howling, screaming, and however else we allow our pain to express itself. Contrary to what we have been conditioned to believe, there is no shame in displaying what we feel with our tears, especially if it assists us in our healing process.

None of us wants to wallow in pain. When loss presents itself, this is the time we must strive to be intentional and disciplined in our personal healing work. Crying is one way, but there are many others. Some find the process of journaling, relying on the support of trusted friends and family, professional counseling, prayer, meditation, exercise, and other healing methods to be helpful. The idea is to clear out any sense of sorrow before it becomes toxic. Restoration allows us to awaken our imagination. In this way, we are able to reconnect with our own inactive dreams, goals, and desires, thereby positioning ourselves for new beginnings.

"Weeping may endure for the night," a time when the light of hope seems dim. In this state of mind, we're unable to see the new opportunity that God has in store for us. The "night" can last a few minutes, hours, days, or weeks, or it can turn into a long dark night of the soul. We must not underrate the value of this stage of recovery, for it prepares us for the joyous outlook toward the dawn of a new day.

Once we've taken the first step back from carrying around the hurt we've been holding, the light of the new day begins to peer through the fog of our pain, and we can once again imagine a new experience for ourselves. As our mourning fades, our joy rises. Whatever tough experiences we face, we can make the choice to move beyond them mentally and emotionally. The dawning of a new day brings with it a new idea, a new perspective, and a new goal for which to strive. In the morning, hope rises like the sun climbing out of the darkness of night. We feel alive again and ready to transcend our circumstances toward the grand possibilities that lie ahead. Having survived a mental cleansing, our imaginations are restored. The creative power of the mind begins to flicker with hope-filled images that beg for our attention.

We may be led back to an unfulfilled dream that has lain dormant. Like an old pair of shoes carefully stored away for many years, dreams may be out of sight but ready and waiting to be worn, used, and rescued from inactivity. Dancing shoes represent the revival of dreams, stimulation of the imagination, awakened creativity. When we reconnect with what brings us joy, the dreams that have longed for our time and attention are standing by and eager for a chance at resurrection, an opportunity to dance once again in our hearts and minds.

One of the good things about unfulfilled dreams is that they hold no grudge or complaint for our long periods of inattention. Instead, they simply live in sweet surrender to the detours we choose along the way. They lie in wait for the day when something will trigger the awakening of what we once imagined. In the nights of our weeping, our unfulfilled dreams hold a silent prayer that they will be rediscovered in the light of a new day.

Extraordinary Step to Empower Your Sole's Journey

Dare to put your imagination toward reclaiming the dream that has been patiently waiting in the closet of your mind. Then celebrate the joy of resurrecting your heart's passion and true desire.

If the Shoe Fits . . .

- What challenges have you faced that inspired you to chart a new course for your life, revive an old dream, imagine a new direction?
- Select a pair of shoes in your closet you've had for an extended period. Are you still going for the same dreams and desires you had when you bought them? Decide if you still want or need to keep them or if it's time to replace them.
- What unfulfilled dreams do you have stored away in the closet of your mind? Why haven't you revived them?
- What is the connection between living your dreams and the expression of joy?
- What would be an Extraordinary Step forward in the use of your *imagination* at this time in your life?

3

A Man and His Gators

H E DIDN'T JUST WALK INTO the room; it came alive when he
entered. One could not help but wonder what made his walk
vibrate like the beat and rhythm of an African drum and the opening
of Beethoven's Fifth Symphony all at the same time. The eyes of those
present started at his head and leisurely fell to his feet. With each step
he took, curiosity mounted in the minds of those who were blessed to
be witnesses. What manner of man walks with such confidence? Some
called it style. Some called it sex appeal. Those who had no frame of
reference for this man's level and display of poise simply marveled at
his presence. His chocolate-colored suit was surely tailor made, for it
was a grand complement to what appeared to be a perfectly sculpted
physique.

But it was his shoes that seemed to add to the stride that called
attention to his swagger. Some men walk in ways that imitate others—
the highest form of flattery—and this man executed each step with the
kind of precision that would surely compel other men to want to copy
his moves. Watching him in motion was intoxicating. Each person
in the room was under his spell—men with envy and women with
fantasy.

Some men underestimate the statement made by a pair of well-designed shoes, but not this man. Some select their suit first and then search for shoes to match; this man most likely did the opposite. With the flair of a Hollywood fashion designer and a magician's touch, he cleverly perfected a unique ensemble that had class written all over it. He oozed charisma. He displayed a flawless unification of masculinity, elegance, and grace. His steps were slow and deliberate, giving every onlooker plenty of time to enjoy a full-body once-over several times before he made his way across the room in his alligator shoes.

Every woman in the room was probably praying the same prayer: *Dear God, let me be the one he'll ask to dance.* Of course, he could ask only one woman at a time, at least that was what everyone assumed. But this man was clearly no ordinary man, so nothing about him should have been taken for granted.

He walked up to a young woman who appeared to be in her midthirties and extended his hand. Her whole face beamed. She glanced around at the women sitting near her just to make sure they all saw that she was the one. But she wasn't "the one." He took her hand, led her to the dance floor, and paused a moment to look her in the eye as though sending her a telepathic message. She was obviously surprised at whatever she interpreted as his message because her expression changed briefly. In the next moment, everyone in the room witnessed the unthinkable, and he did what no one could have predicted—he turned and walked away. He left Number One waiting on the dance floor while he walked into another crowd of hopeful women and selected dance partner Number Two.

She smiled as if she were the first. Just like Number One, she turned to the women close by to assure they were all watching. He courteously extended his hand and proceeded to guide her to the dance floor. He gracefully placed her next to Number One as though he were placing trophies on a shelf. He greeted Number One with a nod and a smile, and then he looked into the face of Number Two. Whatever she determined from his look seemed to be fine with her; she never changed the wide grin on her face. In fact, she seemed happy to have been selected no matter what the details. Number Two stood proudly next to Number One.

However, Mr. Alligator Shoes hadn't finished picking his dance partners. He went on to carefully select four additional women to dance with him, treating each as if she were the only one. After Number Six was in place, Michael Jackson's "Billy Jean" began to play in the background. At first, the man moved his body very slowly. He seemed to anticipate each note before it was heard, as if he had composed the song himself. Attention vacillated between his upper body gestures and the movement of his feet, and then his steps commanded the spotlight. His shoes were now fully on display. They were perfect for dancing, allowing him to turn with precision on a pivot from woman to woman without breaking his rhythm. Every step was brilliant and classy.

Each partner, beautiful and well dressed, seemed to be savvy on the dance floor in her own right. The not-so-ordinary man had selected six extraordinary women for his exceptional display of sagacity. They all seemed to be honored to be included in the exhibition of pure sophisticated pleasure. Although it appeared that the women had been randomly selected from the crowd, there was a synchronization of energy and an unspoken bond between the six of them. The women were respectful of each other, coordinating their moves as if it were part of a choreographed presentation. They all seemed secure in their roles, more than fine with sharing the man who treated them as a florist would handle half a dozen roses each carefully selected for an exquisite bouquet. Those who looked on now knew even more about Mr. Alligator Shoes. He had excellent taste in women, and he knew how to treat them.

All eyes were upon the seven. No others dared set foot upon the dance floor so as not to compete with this public display of boldness and beauty. Every man watching envied Mr. Alligator Shoes' audacity; every woman watching celebrated it. When the music ended, the energy in the room seemed to pause. The collective breath in the room was on hold. What would happen next?

Like a perfect gentleman, the man took the arm of Number Six, then extended his other arm to Number Five. He escorted both of them back to the place from which he'd recruited them. Then, with Number Four on one arm, he extended the other to Number Three. The women seemed to know to wait for him to return them to their seats. Just when all were comfortable with his routine, he broke the pattern of returning two at a time. He left Number One standing on the dance floor as he escorted Number Two back to the group of women, who were cheering and clapping.

A new song started to play. The music encouraged a few couples onto the dance floor. It was a slow song, Nat King Cole singing "Unforgettable." Number One waited patiently, for *what* no one was sure. And then Mr. Alligator Shoes strolled across the dance floor. He moved in close to Number One (who was now The Only), gently placed his right hand around her waist, and extended his left arm. She accepted his gesture and the two began to move. It was as though their bodies had been made for each other; they were in perfect sync. They moved as if they were born to showcase ballroom dancing at that exact moment in time. The other couples on the dance floor abandoned their efforts. They seemed compelled to watch, take notes, or simply be entertained. Every eye in the room followed along as if watching an artist paint a masterpiece on a blank canvas. Every move seemed spontaneous, yet perfectly ordered. They *owned* the dance floor, leaving no space untouched by the soles of their shoes. He pulled her even closer and the two became one without missing a beat.

And just as he walked in the room, so did he leave. He returned Number One to her seat, nodded his head, gave her a half smile, and headed toward the door. Some wanted to know more about the man who had taken command of the room without force or coercion. Every step he made screamed *charm, poise,* and *confidence*, while every movement and gesture simultaneously whispered *talent, skill,* and *personal inner power.* The man with the alligator shoes had touched every person who watched that night in a unique way. And yet he never said a word, and no one even knew his name.

Sole Thoughts

For as he thinks in his heart, so is he . . .
PROVERBS 23:7

You've probably heard it said that action speaks louder than words. The truth of this statement stands out in situations where there are no words exchanged yet something powerful is communicated. While words are informational, they can distract attention from outer appearances. In the absence of words, we direct our attention to others by observing their facades. We may notice the walk, gestures, posture, style of dress, and fit of the clothing, leading us to form some kind of opinion regarding another person. It's among the first impressions we have, but there is more to an individual than meets the eye.

It is easy to surmise that Mr. Alligator Shoes had been intentional and deliberate about how he presented himself. His clothing vibrated luxury and fine taste. His alligator shoes suggested a certain level of prosperity and elegance. His walk projected an air of self-confidence. He made a statement of boldness and style without ever saying a word. Mr. Alligator Shoes obviously knew that appearance matters. However, it was obvious that he also valued his interior qualities as much as his exterior exhibition of fashion and grace.

Mr. Alligator Shoes delivered on the confidence that his physical appearance alluded to. Everything about his outer form revealed that he had taken great care to project a persona of charm and distinction. But we can surely believe that he had also done some inner work that afforded him a solid measure of self-esteem, backed up with the talent and skill of an exceptional dancer. Any dancer would tell us that it takes great discipline, practice, and confidence to carry off a brilliant performance. And still he projected another inner quality. While his methods were daring and unorthodox, he carried himself as a perfect gentleman, a value that speaks to a high level of respect for self and others.

Mr. Alligator Shoes wasn't part of some dress-for-success ploy. At some point, he had taken the time to cultivate the attitude and expertise to back up his public image. He had the moves to support his exceptional display of elegance. He had tapped into his own inner power and brought forth authentic self-confidence, then carefully crafted his outer image to complement his inner character. He had discovered that self-confidence is an inside job, and disciplined his thoughts in a masterful way that gave his talent and skill a legitimate foundation.

We build self-confidence into the core and fiber of who we are in two ways: directly or indirectly. When we intentionally direct our thoughts and words in positive ways, we become masters of our inner world. When we hold high-quality thoughts about ourselves, and for ourselves, we lay the groundwork for inner and outer personal growth. Our positive way of thinking will then influence our actions. In this way, it can be said that our actions reflect the deeper beliefs we have about ourselves, others, and life, "for as he thinks in his heart, so *is* he."

The indirect method is something called "Fake it till you make it." And while this approach is popular as a valid success strategy, it has its drawback. The inspiring idea behind faking it is that in the meantime, we wisely and consciously develop whatever it takes to make it. The key to successfully using this system is not to linger too long in fake-it mode. It is all too easy to become stuck in methods that prove to be nothing more than an outer fashion statement or an ego-driven caricature of self, with little inner substance. The risk is that we limit ourselves to postures that lack the ability to know and express our authentic selves. When our success is based on outer packaging alone, we make a shallow display of ourselves, and the truth can only be hidden for so long before it surfaces.

Appearance *is* important. However, it is just one aspect of how we form opinions about others, and vice versa. We empower our expression of personal attractiveness and style when we learn and practice habitual positive thoughts driven by respect for self and others. This level of expression takes mental and spiritual effort that each of us must do for ourselves, within ourselves. The portrait inside a picture frame holds the value of a work of art, yet both the picture and the frame affect the overall appeal and the price assigned to it. With every effort we make to bring into alignment our authentic *inner* with our legitimate *outer*, we stand to present an extraordinary display of personal power that demonstrates the best of who we are.

Extraordinary Step to Empower Your Sole's Journey

Craft the personal appearance and outer environment that celebrate the inner power, talents, skills, and abilities you've attained through the discipline of your thoughts, words, and actions.

If the Shoe Fits . . .

- In what ways have you worked to discipline your thoughts and words toward developing your inner power?
- When you "dress to impress," what inner preparation do you make to carry the impression beyond outer appearance?
- Do you have a comfortable pair of shoes that also happens to be stylish? How do you feel when you wear them?
- Describe someone you know who has tapped into his or her personal power and who exhibits what appears to be an "authentic" sense of self, with legitimate talents and skills.
- What would be an Extraordinary Step in your life right now toward harnessing your authentic personal *power*?

4

Stilettos

"Liz, you still haven't told us anything about this guy."

"Neicy, keep your voice down, please. I don't want everybody in this shoe store knowing my business," Liz said.

"Well, she *is* right. You haven't told us where you met him, what he does, what he looks like, nothing. Why so secretive?" asked Vanessa, the third of the four women huddled around several pairs of shoes.

"I'm not being secretive." Liz looked at each of her three friends. "I'm just, well, I—"

Neicy interrupted. "Spit it out, girl. What's up?"

Vanessa leaned into the group and whispered, "He must be married."

Neicy's voice elevated. "Oh my God, are you kidding me? Didn't I teach you anything? With all the heartache I went through with Tim, you would even think of going out with a married man?"

"Keep your voice down, please," Liz repeated.

"He couldn't be married. She'd never do that," the fourth woman, Kay, said in a loving, concerned tone. "Liz, talk to us. Say something."

They were all silent as a sad look took over Liz's face. The women moved in closer to her. Neicy stood on her left and put her arm around her, Vanessa took her right hand, and Kay stood in front of her. They waited.

Finally, Kay understood. She looked directly into Liz's face and said with her soft voice, "It's your first date since Dave died. That's it, isn't it?"

Not waiting for her response, Neicy asked, "Is that it? Is that why you've been so quiet about this whole thing? Don't you—"

Vanessa jumped in. "Neicy, be quiet. Can't you see she's hurting?"

They were all quiet for a moment. The three young women looked at Liz for a time, then at each other, trying to figure out what to say next.

Liz finally broke the silence. "It's been five years since Dave died, and I haven't been on a single date. I didn't want to be with anyone after Dave. For a long time, I just didn't feel ready." She paused, looked at her friends, and then continued. "Now, I think . . . maybe . . . I'm ready, but I'm so afraid."

"Why are you afraid?" Kay asked.

"Well, look what happened to the last guy I loved—he died. Maybe something's wrong with me. Maybe I should—"

"Liz, listen to me." Kay moved in closer and added, "Dave would want you to be happy."

"I know he would," Liz said. "It's just that I'm not sure what to say on a date. I haven't been on one in fifteen years. Before I met Dave, all the first dates I'd had were awkward. I don't even remember how to be with anyone other than Dave. I haven't been with another man since my junior year in college. What if he doesn't like me?" Liz paused, seemingly to collect her thoughts. "What if I fall for him and he doesn't fall for me?" She forced a brave half smile, hoping to mask the depth of her fears. "Dave and I were so close. I know he loved me, and I loved him. I wonder if I could ever love someone again." She looked down to avoid eye contact with her friends.

Neicy could no longer hold her words. "Look, girlfriend, we all loved Dave. He was a good man, and yes, he loved you very much, but it's time for you to let him go. I can't believe it's been five years. Oh my God, five long years. Are you telling me it's been five years since—"

Vanessa interrupted. "Liz, sweetie, listen to me. There's nothing wrong with you. Dave was a great guy, but you deserve to have someone in your life. It's time to move on with your life. It's time for you to give yourself permission to be happy again. I know—"

"So it's really been five years?" Neicy blurted out. "You mean to say all these years, you never—"

Kay cut in. "Is he a nice guy?"

"Yeah, he works in my building," Liz replied. "We've run into each other a few times. He's a computer engineer, divorced, no kids. We like a lot of the same things."

"Is he cute?" Neicy asked.

"I think so," Liz said with a slight smile.

"Then listen to me," Kay said. "You'll be fine. Go out with him once, and if he treats you well, go out with him again. Don't make this anything but an opportunity to have a nice time with a nice guy."

"Where's he taking you?" Vanessa asked.

"Some new Thai restaurant downtown."

"Hmm, I heard that's a nice place . . . and expensive too," Neicy said.

"You can do this," Kay assured Liz. "You can get beyond your fear. You know you can. You're strong, Liz. You're the strongest of all of us. I don't know what I'd do if something happened to Lewis or the baby. You've been through a tough time and look at you. You're still beautiful, classy, smart, and fun."

"Kay's right," Vanessa said. "You deserve to be happy again. Dave would give you his blessing; you know he would."

"They're both right," Neicy added. "But more important than all that, no woman as attractive, smart, and funny as you are should ever have to say those pitiful words."

"What pitiful words?" Kay asked.

"It's been five years since I've been on a date," Neicy replied.

Laughter broke out among the women for the first time since they'd been together that day.

Liz had called each of the girls just two days prior and asked them to meet her. When she told them she had a date, they decided to meet at their favorite shoe store when Neicy said a new pair was definitely in order. The four women had been friends since their college days and had shared much joy and pain over the years. They had been with Liz at Dave's funeral and vowed to be a support for her no matter what. But the previous two years had been busy for the four friends; their careers and family life had interfered with the close connection they once had. The call from Liz brought them together for the first time in over a year.

"Ladies," Vanessa said, "we haven't been together like this since Kay's baby shower. I mean, I haven't even seen a picture of little Aaron. I don't even know if he's walking or anything."

"Yes," Kay said, "he's walking and getting into everything."

"You're right," Neicy said as she took Kay's hand. "I haven't seen the baby's pictures either. I'm sorry, Kay. We used to be on top of things like this. We've lost touch with each other, and we have to do better."

"We're your friends, and we let you down," Vanessa said, looking at Liz. "You needed us, and we just weren't there for you. I for one won't let that happen again." She paused and made eye contact with Neicy and Kay. "We all have to make a commitment to make time to meet more often."

"Group hug?" Kay suggested in a tearful voice. A long embrace between the women seemed to draw a bit of attention from the other customers in the store.

The saleswoman who had been helping them leaned into the group and asked in a whisper, "Excuse me, ladies, is everything all right?"

"Nothing that these can't fix." Neicy handed the saleswoman a beautiful bright red four-inch stiletto, then pointed to Liz. "Our friend here is about to break her five-year dry spell. We're going to need these in a size eight."

Sole Thoughts

For God has not given us a spirit of fear,
but of power and of love and of a sound mind.
2 TIMOTHY 1:7

Fear is the enemy of positive advancement in our lives. If we allow it to, it can keep us in a paralyzed state for many years, causing precious moments to pass us by. Fear is not our natural state. But should we temporarily lose our way and wander onto this challenging path, we have a built-in remedy to help us get back on track. That remedy is activated when we remember that our Creator did not give us a spirit of fear but fashioned us with power, love, and a sound mind. It is a blessing to know that we have been endowed with all we need to meet the changes in our lives and avoid getting stuck in the circumstances that bind us to crippling fears.

At some point in time, we will all have to deal with the kind of letting go required to face change in our lives. Sometimes it's a slow and challenging process. Clogging our thinking with mounds of regret and inner turmoil makes it easy for us to be lured into an abyss of fear and stagnation. For a time, we may live under the false impression that we have a viable place to hide, not realizing that the longer we hibernate in the cave of fear, the more difficult the journey back to wholeness.

With change comes the need to renounce the hold the past may have on us so that we are available for the next blessing life has in store. So God gave us the ability to let go of what is finished so we can prepare for the good ahead. We access that inner ability by eliminating the thoughts that keep us stuck in the endless loop of "the way things were" and "why they're not anymore."

This is the time to embrace an attitude that God never gives us more than we can handle or leaves us without resources to meet every experience. We may need support in arriving at this level of belief, however, when we do we realize that we have what it takes to let go of whatever we have been afraid to release. It may be helpful to sort through the good memories we want to keep and the ones we need to set free. This will assist us in shifting our focus from the past and prepare us to discover the hidden pearl lodged in the shell of every change. Keeping the good memories gives us something to hold on to so we can honor what used to be and release the attachment to what might have been. The pearl embedded in every change longs to be set free from the confinement of its shell, but the work required is our own. Great value lies in the ability to accept that new experiences await us and long to become our future memories. What's required of us is that we continually make room in our hearts and minds for the hidden treasurers that can only be found in our willingness to face change.

Moving past worn-out feelings of trepidation puts us in a positive frame of mind, allowing us to avoid a life of dread and fear. We feel God's favor when we make a conscious decision to give up fear. A sound mind exists when there's peace with change. We acknowledge that things happen. Life cannot stand still; it moves, grows, and evolves. There will be times when we are shaken for a moment, but we soon pick up the task of sifting through what is error and what is truth. When we are aware of our God-given power, fear is a temporary visitor in an unwelcoming land.

When we are on the shaky grounds of change, navigating the potholes of fear beneath our feet may not be the easiest experience. One of our most important breakthroughs, however, emerges when we recognize that our Creator has provided many avenues down which we may walk toward our blessings. Every time we take off the shoes we wore traveling a long and hard path of fear, we position ourselves for a new approach in the direction of our hearts' longing. A bright red four-inch pair of stilettos is clearly a bold and uplifting statement of intent and desire to move forward fearlessly. The point is that with the conscious decision to shed what is done, we put on a bright new attitude signaling that our former walk of fear shall become a new stride of courage and self-confidence.

No pair of shoes has the magic power to help us shift from fear to personal courage. What we do on the outside is a reflection of what we think, feel, and believe on the inside. Our work is always relative to how we mentally, emotionally, and spiritually perceive the events of our lives. There may be times when we need assistance in overcoming our fear of letting go, whether it's by seeking some type of professional counseling, joining a support group, or calling on caring friends. When we rely on our inner spirit of power, we find ourselves in the right place at the right time to receive the support we need, even if it's in a shoe store surrounded by loving friends. That's when a new pair of bright red stilettos can feel like magic!

Extraordinary Step to Empower Your Sole's Journey

Trust that God has provided you with all you will ever need to meet every experience, whether it's letting go of the past, fearlessly living in the present, or courageously stepping into a new beginning.

If the Shoe Fits . . .

- Can you recall a time when you were so crippled with fear that you had difficulty moving forward? Describe how you felt. How did you grow from the experience?
- What is it that makes "letting go" difficult?
- Recall a situation where you helped someone else face his or her fears? What did you do?
- Did you ever buy a new pair of shoes for a specific occasion? What was the occasion? How did it turn out for you? Where are those shoes now?
- What would be an Extraordinary Step toward the *release* of some fear you've been holding on to?

shoe shine

THE FATHER TRAVELED A LOT, so the little time he spent with his son was precious to the boy, who craved his father's attention. The father, like many, wanted to provide the best he could for his family, and that meant working long hours during the week and sometimes on weekends as well. This story begins on the boy's thirteenth birthday, a day the boy would never forget.

"Get dressed, son."

"Where are we going, Dad?"

The father handed his son a shoebox. "Here, put these on."

"New shoes? For me? Thanks, Dad!" The boy's face lit up with a wide grin. It was the first time his father had given him a pair of shoes, and it had been a long time since he'd invited him to go someplace with him alone.

The boy ripped open the shoebox and pulled out a black dress shoe. He looked at it for a moment and then pulled the other shoe from the box. "These are great, Dad. They're just like yours."

"Good. Glad you like them, son. Now go upstairs and put them on with your dress slacks."

"The ones I wear to church?" the boy asked.

"Yeah."

"Okay! But where are we going?"

"You gonna stand here and question me," the father said, "or do you want to go with me?"

"I want to go with you. I'll be ready in a few minutes." The boy grabbed the shoes and the empty box and then ran up the stairs and out of his father's sight.

"And put on a nice shirt too," the father yelled up the stairway.

"What's going on?" asked a young girl as she peeked her head in the boy's room.

"Man stuff," the boy said proudly. "You wouldn't understand."

"You goin' somewhere?"

"Yeah, I'm going with Dad."

"Where?" The girl looked down and blurted out, "Hey, you've got new shoes."

"Yep, birthday present from Dad. Cool, right?"

"I guess. But where's he taking you?"

"Not sure," the boy answered.

The girl turned and ran down the stairs, her plaits bouncing with excitement. "Dad, where you goin'? Can I go too?"

"Not this time, angel," the man said as he hugged her and then patted her on the head.

"Hey up there, let's get a move on!" the father yelled.

The boy appeared, pausing at the top of the stairs as if taking in a historic moment. With one step at a time, he slowly started to descend the stairs. It was a walk that screamed, *Hey, look at my new shoes!* He knew that new shoes had to be tested first, and he gave them his best test walk. He seemed to savor the first steps in his new shoes. By the time he was halfway down, his mother had joined his sister and father at the foot of the stairs. The mother's face revealed that a proud moment was indeed taking place.

"My, my, my, don't you look handsome," she said.

"We'll be back by dinnertime," the man said as he planted a soft kiss on his wife's forehead before walking out the door.

As a tease to his little sister, the boy gently kissed her on the forehead. "Don't wait up. The menfolk will be out for a while." He followed his father out the door.

The father was mostly silent on the drive to their undisclosed location, but that didn't stop the boy from talking almost constantly.

"Thanks for the shoes, Dad. They fit perfect."

The father reacted with a slight smile and a nod.

"The size is just right for me, and they feel great," the boy persisted.

"That's great, son."

"Where are you taking me, anyway?"

"Just relax."

"Are we almost there?"

Just then, the father pulled over to park. The boy looked around for some indication of their destination.

"We're there?" the boy asked.

"Yep, this is it."

The boy got out of the car slowly, still searching for clues. The mystery ended as his father walked up to the door marked CHARLEY'S SHOE SHINE.

"Come on, son. Today you're going for your first shoe shine."

From that moment on, the boy watched his father for hints in appropriate behavior for getting a shoe shine. There were several vacant chairs in the small but clean shop. The father headed toward a particular chair and then motioned to his son to take the chair next to his. The boy listened to his father talking with the man named Charles, the owner of the shop. They seemed to have a rapport, the kind the boy wished he had with his father.

"Charles, this is my son. It's his thirteenth birthday."

"Thirteen?" Charles said. "My, oh my, the time does go by. It's been many years since I saw him last. He extended his hand toward the boy and gave him a firm handshake. "Happy birthday, young man."

"Thanks."

"I thought it about time for him to have his first shine," the father said.

"Hey, John, come on out here," Charles yelled over the sound of jazz playing through the large overhead speakers. "We've got a young man who's here for his first shine."

A young man emerged from behind a curtained-off area. He appeared to be just a boy himself.

John looked at the boy seated in the chair, nodded a hello, and immediately began putting polish on his shoes. The boy wanted to talk to John, just as his father was talking with Charles. But listening to his father's conversation about politics and business, he realized that he couldn't talk about these subjects. However, the urge to have a conversation was too great to let the opportunity pass by without trying.

"How long you been working here?" the boy asked.

"Since I was twelve," John replied without looking up.

"How old are you now?"

"Seventeen."

"Well, you seem to be really good at what you do."

"Thanks."

"Yeah, so now that I'm thirteen, I'm going to be looking for a job real soon." The boy paused, hoping for some response from John. Finally, he asked, "How did you get this job?"

The boy had finally asked the right question. John looked up.

"This is my dad's shop. He taught me to shine, like his father before him," John said with pride.

"He's your father?" the boy asked with surprise, pointing at Charles.

"Yep, that's my dad." John paused and nodded in Charles's direction. "When he opened this shop, I was just a kid, but he let me come here on the weekends to help clean up and stuff. Then when I turned twelve, he started letting me shine a little. I didn't like it at first; I just wanted to hang out with my dad. But it's okay now; it's not so bad."

For the first time all day, the boy had nothing to say. He looked over at Charles shining his father's shoes and then back at John as he was busy shining his shoes. They shined shoes alike, and they even looked alike. He looked at his own father and watched him laughing and talking with Charles. He saw a side of his father he hadn't seen before—truly enjoying a conversation. He had thought his father was a man of few words, but the man next to him now seemed to be a different man, someone he wanted to get to know better. He wondered if he would ever be as close to his father as John seemed to be to his.

Charles completed his work. The boy watched as his father stood and looked at his shoes. "Thanks, man, you've done it again. This is why I drive across town—you're the best."

Charles had a big grin on his face, proud of his work. The two men engaged in some light banter, and there was more laughter.

John hurried to finish his work. The boy stood up and looked at his shoes just as his father had.

"Thanks John, you did a great job. I hope my dad will bring me back again."

The father reached into his wallet, pulled out what looked to be two new bills—a twenty and a five—and handed them to Charles.

"Hey, man, I appreciate you," Charles said.

Still taking mental notes on the whole experience, the boy wondered about the price of the shoe shine and how much the tip was. He figured there must have been a big tip because Charles's grin grew even wider than before. Then his father went into his wallet again, pulled out a five-dollar bill, and handed it to his son. "Give this to John. He did a good job on your shoes."

The boy was awkward giving the money to John, who took it and smiled for the first time.

"Thanks for the tip," John said.

The two men engaged in what looked like a secret handshake and then looked each other in the eye. "Two weeks?" Charles asked.

"You know it. Take care of yourself and give my best to Helen."

Then John, following his father's lead, extended his hand toward the boy. They shook hands like their fathers, minus the secret handshake.

On the drive home, the boy couldn't help but notice a change in his father's demeanor. He was more upbeat and was still in that talkative mood that had surfaced during his shoe shine.

"How was it, son?"

"It was great, Dad."

"Well, when a young man reaches a certain age, there are things he needs to know."

"I know what you mean," the boy said, trying to sound grown-up. "Now I know how to act when I get a shoe shine."

"Son, this was far more than a lesson on how to act when you get a shoe shine."

"What do you mean?"

The father seemed to choose his words carefully. "I've known Charles for over twenty years. We served in the army together—until he was wounded in combat and then discharged. He and his wife, Helen, came to our wedding when I married your mother. I had a cigar with him the night John was born. When he opened that shoe shine shop, I was his first customer."

"I had no idea," the boy said in a soft voice.

"I don't know a finer man than Charles Jackson the Third. He does do a great shoe shine, but I drive across town twice a month to talk to a man I have great respect for."

"I think I understand," the boy said as he stared at his father.

"I hope so. I've watched Charles recover from some tough times, and he has amazed and inspired me more times than I can count. He even saved me from making some pretty bad decisions more than a few times over the years."

"What do you mean?"

"Well, sometimes a man needs another man to talk to about things. Charles has been there for me, and I've tried to be there for him. Don't be fooled by his work, son. Charles is a wise man."

"What kinds of things, Dad?"

"Life and all the stuff that comes up. Sometimes a man may have a hard time opening up and getting things off his chest. Things he can't tell his wife or sister or mother. What I'm trying to say is that a man needs a safe place to be a man. Sometimes he needs someone who can be the voice of solid reasoning, who understands things only another man would. Someone who understands things beyond the immediate circumstance."

There was an emotional pause. The boy noticed that his father seemed to be reflecting on something that he did not choose to share. They traveled for a few miles in silence.

Finally, the father broke the silence. "If anything should ever happen to me, you can talk to Charles. Think of him as an uncle. Growing up, I always wanted a brother. The day I met Charles, I felt like God had answered my prayer. Son, it's a rare experience, but sometimes God puts people in our lives who . . . well, you just know you're going to be close to them all your days. That's how it was when I met your mother, and that's how it was when I met Charles. I hope you find a few close people to share your life with the way I have."

"But what are you saying? Is something wrong?"

"No, no, son. It's just that Charles and I made a pact when we were in the army. We said that if we ever had kids and something happened to one of us, well . . . Just remember Charles Jackson is a man you can trust. I've trusted him with my life many times, and he's trusted me with his." The father paused and glanced over at his son, whose eyes were fixed on him. "If ever I'm not around, promise me you'll stay in touch with Charles. Will you remember that?"

"Yes, Dad. I will."

The silence in the car this time was longer than the first. The upbeat mood from the shoe shine experience had faded. The boy said softly, "John seems pretty cool too. He told me his dad taught him how to shine when he was twelve."

"Charles is devoted to his family, a good husband and good father to all four of his children." The man smiled to himself. "John is the oldest and the only boy. Charles was so proud when he was born. His wife had a rough time delivering him, and Charles was right there the whole time. He never left her side."

"Can I tell you something?"

"Sure. I hope you always feel that you can talk to me."

"At first I was a little jealous of how close Charles and John seem to be. When John told me his dad taught him how to shine, I wondered if you would ever teach me about your work someday." There was another emotional pause, and then the boy continued. "But I realize that you've already taught me a lot of stuff."

"Son, you, your mother, and your little sister mean everything to me. That's why I've worked so hard. I know I haven't spent a lot of time at home, but I've tried to make sure that no matter what, my family will be taken care of. All I've ever wanted was to provide a good life for you all." The man extended his hand and patted his son's knee. "I love you. Remember that."

Suddenly, a truck slammed into the left side of the car. When he regained his awareness, the boy could hear sirens and people talking. There was a woman standing over him. "Can you hear me?" she was asking repeatedly.

"Where's my dad?" The boy tried to turn his head to look around.

"Just calm down, son," the woman said. "There's been an accident."

"I don't see my dad. I want to see my dad."

A week later, Charles Jackson III spoke at the funeral to the nearly two hundred people who gathered to pay their respects. "Who among us holds the wisdom to know the true meaning of life and death? Certainly not me. I feel like my friend's life was too short. I know he would agree because he recently told me he wanted to start spending more time with his family, and on the day he died, he had begun to do just that." Charles paused to compose himself. "However, God has bigger plans and greater knowledge than we can even conceive of. Today we are all painfully aware that the time we spend in this lifetime is precious. It seems to come in a blink of an eye and leave just as quickly."

Charles paused again and then cleared his throat. "Twice a month for the last fifteen years, my most loyal customer came to see me under the guise of wanting a shoe shine. He could have gone to get a shoe shine from two or three shops he had to pass to get to me. He paid me more than I charged and tipped me far too generously. Some Saturdays I felt like I should have been the one tipping him, for he was my greatest teacher. He challenged me to think about things in a way that no one else did. Because of how he chose to spend his time every other Saturday, I am a better friend, husband, father, and businessman. My prayer today is that he knew I loved him like a brother; my regret is that I never told him so. Now I'm challenged to make good use of the new time slot created in my schedule every second and fourth Saturday, a slot I will hold open for his son if he will accept it. In closing, let me just say that even in death, my friend is still teaching me lessons about life. What I have learned from the untimely loss of my longest friendship is not to put off saying 'I love you,' and to make an effort to spend as much quality time with family, friends, and loved ones as possible in the seemingly limited number of days that God grants us."

Sole Thoughts

To everything there is a season, a time for every purpose under heaven.
ECCLESIASTES 3.1

Time is life's most curious gift. While every moment of every day is a present from our Creator, at some point on our journey, we will arrive at the moment when the gift must be surrendered. Most of us will admit that we do not have a clear understanding of why, how, and when the measurement of minutes, days, weeks, or years must concede to the greater plan. But even though we have no conscious knowledge of how long we shall have access to all that life has to offer, we are expected to enjoy the gift for as long as we have it. Still, not knowing how much time we have is not an excuse to spend energy looking over our shoulder for the Grim Reaper to creep up on us. The gift of time has been loaned to us so that we might use every ounce, portion, and dimension of it to meet every challenge and opportunity that confronts us—with faith, courage, and poise—even to the appointed time we call death.

So we find ourselves with a tremendous gift yet also in a precarious situation. Each individual must arrive at his or her own understanding of this gift of time. Ironically, we may spend years or even decades trying to figure out how to appreciate, use, and enjoy this great gift. We're challenged with the responsibility of discovering how to live in a way that balances work, family, recreational activities, friendships, personal interests, and our spiritual growth while making the most of the many opportunities we encounter along the way. This balancing act is filled with life lessons of various kinds according to "every event under heaven." The level at which we discern and implement our own value-based priorities determines the true significance of our days. And yes, when the appointed time demands that we yield to the end of our trek in this life, those we leave behind will be challenged with understanding why—and most likely question their own use and appreciation of time.

In our search for answers, we may examine how fully our loved one lived, or how wisely we think he or she spent the time available to them. For many of us, when we think of receiving a gift, our minds tend to go to the material. Unfortunately, sometimes it takes the absence of someone we love before we realize the value of our days as a great nonmaterial gift. We discover too often that relationships end with the pain of regret and wish we'd had more quality time with those who are gone from us. We may even regret that we said what was on our minds but neglected to say what was on our hearts. Often times it is after the fact, that we realize there is great wisdom in seizing the opportunities life gives us to balance head and heart.

The boy in the story will probably never forget his thirteenth birthday. The new shoes will be remembered as the last material gift his father gave him. The father gave the son his first pair of grown-up shoes, symbolizing the role he was about to assume that would require strength and maturity beyond the boy's years. New shoes suggest support for the new steps the boy will take going forward into uncharted territory marked with unknown responsibilities. But the father also left the son with still another gift—a shoe shine.

A shoe shine removes the dust and particles we collect as we journey through life. It restores the look of the shoes, the shine representing a light on the path going forward. The boy's first shoe shine was important, not so much for the shoe shine itself—his shoes were new. It was an experience in, and an example of, spending quality time nurturing and developing relationships. The light of wisdom unveiled an important lesson about the value of a support system, friendship, and having a safe place to share thoughts and feelings. The father wanted his son to know that there would be times when he would need those things, and he left his son with the knowledge of one possible setting where he could find them . . . and a person he could trust in the process.

The legacy we leave to loved ones is like a double-sided coin. One side is the wisdom and knowledge we impart to them with our words and by the example of how we live our lives. It may sound a bit morbid at first, but it is a great act of love to leave this lifetime knowing that we have equipped our loved ones with tools to survive and recover from tough times, even our own death. The legacy could be anything from leaving a last will and testament, a living trust, orderly instructions on distribution of personal property, a list of things we neglected to say, and gratitude notes, to where and how to get the emotional, mental, physical, or spiritual support needed to heal from feelings of loss.

On the other side of the legacy coin are the good memories of time well spent with others. When we spend quality time with loved ones, our souls are nourished by the love we give, and our loved ones are strengthened by the love they receive. Moments with loved ones where there is an exchange of love and joy are among life's greatest blessings. Embedded in the love we share with others are the skills for healing and the tools to move forward in life.

The wisdom to understand the various facets of life's journey may elude us until it's our unique time to face end-of-life issues. Comfort may be found in looking at what we call death as only a point in an eternal journey, a transition to another dimension of being, rather than the absolute end of existence itself. We leave behind parts of ourselves in the memories others hold of us, the good deeds we planted, and the high-quality time spent with others; in this way, life does not end but continues in a new way.

When your appointed time arrives, let it be said that you did more than use up the time you had—rather, you invested it in the people and projects for which you held great love and ascribed meaning and value. Any of us would be proud to leave this endowment with our loved ones. Knowing that you attained a level of appreciation that allowed you to value time as a precious gift will empower you to walk into the light of transition saying, *Yea, though I walk through the valley of the shadow of death, I will fear no evil . . .* (Psalm 23:4). Some may label your physical exit as the end, but having invested your days wisely in this lifetime, you will leave behind an inheritance that will pay dividends in the lives of those you touched for many years beyond the gift of time God so lovingly paced in your hands.

Extraordinary Step to Empower Your Sole's Journey

Let the light of inner wisdom amplify your respect and value of life's most precious gift—time.

If the Shoe Fits . . .

- What is your understanding of the length of time any of us is granted?
- Do you have a pair of shoes that hold great sentimental value for you? What gives them that great value?
- Who is/are the person/persons you would like to spend more quality time with? Why don't you?
- Do you think the man in the story did justice to the old saying "Treat each day as if it were your last" on his final day? If yes, how? If no, why not?
- Have you prepared your loved ones with what they will need to know when you make your transition? If so, what does this entail?
- What would be an Extraordinary Step toward greater *wisdom* in how you spend and manage your time?

6

Footprints in the Snow

Six-year-old Cassie burst into the kitchen, full of early morning energy. "Mom, it snowed again!"

The woman standing at the stove wore a bathrobe that was tattered and worn. Her salt-and-pepper hair was pulled back from her tired-looking face, upon which she forced a smile. Without looking up from the large pot she was stirring, she responded, "I know, baby."

Cassie was always the first of the four children to come into the kitchen on school days. She was full of enthusiasm and loved spreading her spirit throughout the household. "Well, what am I going to do?" she asked.

"Put on a double pair of socks." The woman spoke in a soft, loving voice, but she still hadn't looked up from her pot. "Those thick ones I bought for you last week."

"Double socks don't work, Mom. I did that last time, and my feet still got wet," Cassie said.

"Take an extra pair of socks with you, and when you get to school, change into your dry ones."

Cassie seemed satisfied with her mother's solution. "Okay, I'll try it." When she turned to leave with the same energy she had when she entered, she stopped short of bumping into her older sister, who was just walking into the kitchen.

"Mom told me to take an extra pair of socks and change into them when I get to school," Cassie told the older girl, who seemed uninterested in her remark.

"Well, whatever you're going to do, you'd better hurry up. I can't let you make me late again," the older girl said as Cassie rushed past her.

The woman finally looked up from her pot. "Sit so you can eat your breakfast," she said to the older girl.

"Not oatmeal again?" The older girl pouted as she sat down reluctantly at the kitchen table.

"Yes, my dear daughter, oatmeal!" The woman heaped the cereal into a bowl and shoved it in front of the girl. "Eat!"

"Mom, can't I have something else? You know I hate this stuff."

"There will be pancakes Saturday morning. Today it's oatmeal! So eat."

Cassie returned to the kitchen, once again making a lively entrance. "Oatmeal! I love it!" She sat at the table in front of one of four bowls filled with it. She wasted no time and dove right in with a big smile. "Can I put some more sugar on it, Mom?"

"I gave you one teaspoon; that's all you need," the woman said while shaking her head from side to side. "You, little girl, do not need more sugar in your system."

The older girl slowly stirred her oatmeal, obviously with no intention of eating it. She leaned across the table toward Cassie and whispered, "Since you love this stuff so much, you can have mine."

"Okay, that's enough chatter," their mother interrupted. "You girls need to eat up so you can get out of here. Are the boys nearly ready?"

"Don't know," the older girl said, still slowly stirring her food.

"Yeah. I mean, I think so," Cassie said between shoving spoons of oatmeal into her mouth. "I peeked in their room, and they were getting dressed. Do you want me to go check on them?"

"No, young lady, you just take care of yourself. Did you get the extra pair of clean socks and put them in your bag?" the mother asked.

Cassie nodded with her mouth full. "Uh-huh."

At that moment, two boys walked in the kitchen, one high school age, the other elementary school age. Neither of them said a word as they sat down in front of one of the bowls and began to eat.

The mother stood over the table as all four of her children ate, or in the case of the oldest girl, pretended to eat. "It's supposed to snow some more this afternoon," she said as she carefully placed a brown paper bag in front of each of the three youngest children and a few coins in front of the oldest boy. "Make sure you all bundle up when you leave school."

The older boy looked at Cassie. "What you gonna do about the snow, squirt?"

Cassie proudly told him about her solution with the extra socks.

"She'll be fine," the mother said in an assuring tone. "Now off you go. You'll all be late if you don't get a move on, and don't forget your lunches."

"But I'm not finished with my oatmeal," Cassie complained.

"Mom, she's going to make me late again," the older girl protested. "She takes so long to do everything."

The mother looked at Cassie. Without a word, the little girl got up from the table after shoving one last heaping spoon into her mouth. She dashed toward the front door, where her siblings had already begun to dress for another snowy day.

The four put on their winter coats, scarves, hats, and gloves. Three of the four put on boots that had been neatly placed near the door. The mother planted a gentle kiss on the forehead of each of her children as they walked out the door single file.

For each of them, she had a little message. To the oldest girl: "Have a good day—and take care of your little sister."

To the youngest boy: "Behave yourself today, okay?"

To the oldest boy: "Come straight home after school. You'll probably have snow to shovel, and I have a few errands for you to run."

And to Cassie: "Just follow carefully in your sister's footprints and you'll be fine."

Without a word to the girls, the boys took off running through the three inches of freshly fallen snow. The oldest one would see to it that the younger boy arrived safely at the elementary school before he continued on to the high school. Separate dismissal times allowed both boys to walk home from school with their own friends from the neighborhood. There were three schools in the same area—the elementary school, the middle school next to it, and the high school just a block beyond the middle school. Although the youngest boy attended the same school as the girls, he refused to walk with them, saying on occasion, "The men of the family have to stick together."

The girls usually met with friends along the walk to school, except on days when it snowed.

"Don't walk so fast!" Cassie shouted at her sister.

"I don't want to be late. You always slow me down, and then I'm in trouble for being late."

Cassie took each step cautiously. She knew her shoes would get wet like so many times before, but she always hoped she could minimize the damage by being extra careful, and in her mind that meant walking slowly. She meticulously made each step inside the footprint left by her sister in the snow.

The older girl had come up with this strategy when their mother announced that she didn't have money to buy new boots for all of them. Only one of the four children would get new ones for the winter. The obvious choice was the older boy; he was in his senior year in high school. He was outdoors a lot because of his paper route, plus he ran errands for their mother, shoveled the snow, and many times shoveled snow for neighbors so he could earn a little extra money for the household. They all knew who should receive the new boots.

At one of the regular family meetings, the older girl announced a plan to make it all work. "I can wear my boots from last year. They're a little tight, but they'll last another year." She looked at the youngest boy and said, "You'll get his old boots from last year," pointing first to the youngest boy and then to the older. "And you," she said, pointing to Cassie, "walk behind me when it snows." She turned to their mother. "Cassie can walk in my footprints, and that way her shoes won't get so wet." Obviously pleased with her proposal, she lifted up both hands and said, "See? It's a perfect plan."

And her plan worked, only she hadn't counted on the patience required to wait on her little sister.

"Hurry up! I think I just heard the first bell." The older girl stopped and motioned to Cassie, who had fallen behind.

"I'm coming," Cassie called, "but you're taking big steps and going too fast. I'm doing the best I can."

When Cassie finally caught up, the older girl said, "Okay. The walkway to the school has been shoveled, so you don't need me anymore. I'm going ahead so I'm not late."

"You're leaving me!" Cassie called to her sister. The sound of the second bell generated a hurried motion toward the front door from all the latecomers. "I was hoping you'd help me put on my dry socks when I get inside."

The older girl stopped. She could hear their mother's voice in her head: *Take care of your little sister.* She turned around and waited once again for Cassie to catch up. "You are so slow," she said as Cassie approached. She took her little sister's hand, complaining the whole time as they walked toward the door. "We're going to have to go to the principal's office again. I hate going in there. They're probably going to call Mom this time." The third bell rang. "See? I knew it. We're late."

"I'm sorry," Cassie said. "I just didn't want you to leave me." The two girls were silent as they walked through the double doors.

A woman was standing in the hallway waving a line of late children into the room marked TARDY STUDENTS. They would be checked in one at a time. The first-, second-, and third-timers would be told to go join their classes. But for repeat offenders with more than four times, a chat with the assistant principal could be required at the discretion of the attendance monitor. And for those who were tardy more than five or six times, a phone call to the parents was the next step before the student would be allowed to go to class.

"Well, ladies," the woman said to the two girls still holding hands, "so glad you could join us this morning." Looking specifically at the older girl, she said, "I told you last time I would have to call your mother the next time you girls came in late. I had hoped your little chat with the assistant principal would help. I just don't understand why you and your little sister can't get here on time. Think what a terrible example you are setting for her." She glanced over at Cassie and then continued talking to the older girl. "You're going to be moving on to middle school next year, and she's going to follow in your footsteps with this habit of being late."

Cassie held her head down. She stared at her wet shoes. As careful as she had been, water from the snow had still seeped through her shoes. Her feet were cold and wet, but she dared not say a word. She had caused enough trouble for one day, and it was just nine fifteen in the morning.

"Sit." The woman seemed impatient with the older girl. She pointed to the wooden bench against the wall. "Over there."

The two girls, still holding hands, walked over to the bench. They disconnected their hands so they could sit down. Cassie sat close to her sister but did not look at her. She didn't want to see the disappointment that she'd seen when they were late just two days earlier.

"I'm going to call your mother. I'm determined to get to the bottom of this." The woman went into the office with a door that was glass on the top half and wood on the bottom. The girls could see her looking in the files for the phone number, and then they watched her pick up the phone and dial.

The girls sat in silence for what seemed a long time as the woman talked on the phone. She did most of the talking at first, and then she seemed to be listening a lot. A puddle of water had formed below their feet.

Finally, Cassie broke the silence. "I need to change my socks, like Mom said."

Without hesitation, the older girl extended her hand. "Give them to me."

Cassie looked in her small school bag and pulled out a pair of red socks.

"Why do you have red socks, Cassie? They don't match what you have on."

"I know, but I like them. They're my favorite color."

"You are so weird," the older girl said as she kneeled before her sister. She took off the wet shoes and soggy socks and laid them to the side. She put the red socks on Cassie's feet.

As Cassie looked on, she said, "Next year when I get new boots, you won't have to wait for me." She was silent for a second and then said, "And besides, I'll be taller next year, and my legs will be longer, so I can keep up better." She was silent for another second before saying, "Just think—you'll be in middle school next year, and you won't have time for me anyway."

The door opened, and the woman motioned to the girls to come into her office. She stood silent for a moment, looking at the older girl. "Your mother said you take the extra time walking to school to make footprints in the snow for your sister, who doesn't have boots."

"Yes, ma'am." Holding her head down, the older girl began to cry. "I'm supposed to look after my little sister, but she's so slow sometimes."

The woman's tone softened. "How old are you?"

"I'm twelve, but Cassie's only six, so my mom wants me to look after her. I try real hard, but—"

The woman interrupted her. "Well, I think it's good that you take such good care of your little sister. I've seen you with her, and you have great patience. What were you doing out there just before I called you in here?"

"I was changing her socks. Her feet get wet, so my mother told her to put on dry socks when we get indoors."

"You're a good big sister," the woman said as she began to fidget with a pencil she held in her hand. "I know what that's like." She paused for a moment as if recalling her own experience. She appeared a bit emotional when she said, "It can be a little tough. Just do the best you can. It's a huge responsibility to care for your younger siblings, but . . . well . . . sometimes we just have to do what we have to do and hope for the best."

"Yes, ma'am."

"For some of us, it doesn't get any better, but you still have to try." The woman paused again. Her thoughts were clearly somewhere else.

Finally, her attention turned to Cassie. "You, little girl, are going to have to help your sister—after all, she's helping you. Will you try harder to work with her to get here on time?"

Cassie turned to her older sister. "I'm sorry. I'll try to walk faster."

"Now let's get you girls to class."

The next day and the day after that, it snowed. And yes, despite Cassie's best efforts, the girls were late. In fact, every day it snowed that winter, the girls were late for school.

Sole Thoughts

Order my steps . . .
PSALM 119:133 (KJV)

The relationship we have with siblings can be a great blessing, but the relationship also holds great responsibility. Often the older siblings, perhaps without realizing it, help chart the course by which the younger siblings will follow. Some of the most impactful lessons we learned about being in relationships with others can be traced back to our childhood experiences with those who made up our family unit. If there were other children in the house, there was most likely some shared responsibilities among them—for each other. So in addition to our own self-care we may have been charged with caring for siblings as well. However, it is usually much later in life when we realize the influence our early bonds had on shaping our adult lives and relationships.

In our early years, we looked mostly to our caretakers and family members to pave the way for us. We watched and we learned. Sometimes we imitated the actions we saw. We listened to the words they spoke and filed them away in our memory banks for the future. We searched for the how-tos that could help us find our way to live with meaning, value, and purpose.

We welcomed an orderly path that we could follow—footprints to guide the way. They provided us with what we hungered for in those early years: to know we were not alone, and that someone cared enough to invest time and attention to show us the way. We sought the assurance of a systematic process by which we could put one foot in front of the other on a tried and proven path. We followed, trusting that we would not be led astray, expecting to have a chance to survive and perhaps even thrive.

While family members most likely made the first footprints we followed, members of the educational and religious systems may have made those we followed later. Education provides the path by which our minds may be filled with an understanding of math, literature, science, chemistry, and civics so that we are prepared to succeed on life's journey. Educators leave footprints in the minds of their students. If those steps have been honorably and wisely placed, learners will go beyond the paved territory and become pioneers, someday leaving footprints of their own. *I have taught you in the way of wisdom; I have led you in right paths* (Proverbs 4:11).

Religion has the same charge. The children of Israel followed Moses out of slavery and bondage. Jesus told his disciples to follow him. The prophet Muhammad points the way to follow Allah. Religion encourages us to follow proven truths as revealed by God's messengers, who have gone before us on the spiritual path. When we look at the pattern of the various footprints of religious leaders, they seem to be going in different directions, yet most would agree they all lead to one God, though referenced by many names. The footprints they leave activate the faith embedded in our spirits.

As we journey through life, we will find at various points that we are the ones making footprints for others to follow, and at other times, we are the ones following in the steps of another. With the exception of children still in their early developmental stage, followers have the responsibility of discerning whose footprints to follow. We are expected to make mature decisions regarding the direction we tread in our pursuit of health, happiness, and prosperity. Our charge is to give the best of ourselves, whether we are leaving footprints or following them.

Many people willingly take on the role and responsibility of being footprint makers through their profession or volunteer status, such as teachers, counselors, coaches, advisers, spiritual leaders, and mentors.

They impact and influence the lives of others. Their footprints can make an empowering mark on our path in life, influence the greater community, and impact our world.

Whether or not we are conscious of it, whether we desire it or not, we all set an example that others will notice and perhaps imitate. You may declare, "I'm not trying to be anyone else's guide. I'm just living the life I want to live." That position is understandable, but it presents a naive line of thinking. Since none of us live in the world alone, anytime we are within earshot or view of another, there is a possibility that we leave some kind of impression on the hearts and minds of others. To a greater extent, writers, politicians, musicians, teachers, and other professionals who communicate ideas (verbal and nonverbal) have the possibility of influencing others' thinking. So it is important to know that who we are, and how we show up, matters. Yet regardless of the kinds of shoes we wear, or even if we're in our bare feet, all of us are always leaving footprints of some kind.

As we journey through life our willingness to follow footprints placed in our path reveals our gravity toward the idea of order. Just as we appreciate the process of the sun rising in the east and setting in the west every day, so do we welcome assurances of a divinely ordered plan to show us how to live, thrive, and enjoy life. When we see others who appear to be what we hope to be, who have what we would like to have, who live the way we desire to live, we might replicate their moves and hope to get the results they appear to have achieved.

What would the world look like if we all took up the charge of being the best footprint makers we could be? If we set a goal of living with respect, honesty, and integrity, we would leave honorable footprints for others to follow. We would demonstrate that the road to high-quality living is an orderly process of putting one foot in front of the other, so long as the path is the way of wisdom. Surely we would love to say these words to those who follow in our steps: *I have led you in right paths.*

Extraordinary Step to Empower Your Sole's Journey

Leave a path of orderly footprints that speak honorably of who you are and that will be a blessing to all those who are guided to follow them.

If the Shoe Fits . . .

- What orderly systems do you see at work in the world? (Example: the rising and setting of the sun.)
- What orderly systems are at work in your body?
- Looking back over your past, can you identify situations or circumstances that you believe were part of an orderly design or divine plan for your life?
- Who are some of the people who left honorable footprints for you to follow?
- For whom are you leaving honorable footprints? What would you like your footprints to convey to others?
- If you were literally leaving a trail for someone to follow, what type of shoes would you wear, and why?
- Have you ever thanked those in whose footsteps you have followed?
- What would be an Extraordinary Step toward embracing a greater sense of *order* in your life?

7

In His Shoes

S HE TOOK OFF HER FLIP-FLOPS and let the sand caress her toes. A walk on the beach was her way of clearing her mind, especially when she needed time alone to think. She walked toward the cold water, and when the tide came in, she let the water splash all over her body. She quickly ran back to the hot sand, giggling and squealing like a little girl at play. Suddenly, she remembered that she hadn't come to the beach to play. She was a thirty-two-year-old woman who had come to the beach with the hope of washing away her mounting sense of disappointment and fear. The disappointment was in herself. The gut-level ache that kept her from sleeping night after night confirmed that she was about to do something that would only add guilt to her growing disappointment. Carol's fear was that she would do it anyway.

She looked up at the sky to see that it was a beautiful clear blue. It seemed to be a good day to face the dilemma she'd gotten herself into. Her mind drifted back to when she met Brian, and she smiled while reflecting on that day in the coffee shop.

She had passed that coffee shop many times over the past few years, and until that day, not once had she gone in. Carol laughed at the thought of a non-coffee-drinking person feeling drawn to enter a coffee shop. She had ordered a chai tea and a scone and then taken a seat near a window. When she looked over at the next table, she noticed a man staring at her.

"Hi," he said, as though he knew her.

Carol smiled and nodded to him.

"It's nice to see you," he said.

"I'm sorry, have we met?"

"You probably don't remember me, but yes, we have met," he answered.

This man is fine. How could I not remember him? she thought.

He got up from his table and sat across from her. "Dallas. The flight to Dallas."

Carol looked at him with a puzzled expression. "Go on."

"We sat next to each other on a flight about two years ago. You're a teacher, right?"

"Yes, I am," she said. "You're right. Now I remember. You're an architect, and you had just gotten a divorce."

"Yeah, that's right," he said.

"I do remember . . . You have a little boy, right?"

"That's right. And you're married with a daughter."

"Wow," she said, nodding. "What a great memory you have."

"It's hard not to remember someone who changed your life."

"Excuse me?" Carol asked as she leaned forward.

"Well, I must confess that you had a great impact on me that day." He paused and took a sip from his cup. "I mean, the way you listened to me and let me get some of that pain off my chest was exactly what I needed. I hadn't shared my feelings about my divorce with anyone. And there you were, a perfect stranger on an airplane, willing to listen."

"Wow. I don't know what to say . . . except I'm glad I could help."

"I never really got a chance to thank you." He paused, looking down at his cup. "It was a turning point for me. I was able to get on with my life after that day." He paused again and looked up at her. "Thank you." There was an awkward silence while he seemed to be reliving the past.

"Well," Carol said, attempting to lift the somber mood, "I bet you're already happily remarried."

"Happy, yes; remarried, no. I've forgiven my ex, and I get to see my son every other week, so I'm okay. When I met you, my life was a wreck . . . and I was a mess. No wonder you didn't recognize me. What about you? Are you still happily married?"

She smiled and looked down at her cup of tea. "Yes, I'm still married."

He smiled at her response. "So here we are after all this time. I'm glad I ran into you." His watch made a beeping sound. "Oh, I need to get to my office. I'm so glad I ran into you . . . I said that already, didn't I?"

"Yes, you did," she said.

"You know, I don't normally stop in here for coffee but today . . . for some reason . . . I felt drawn here. I think it was fate, like on the flight to Dallas. Well, anyway, it was good . . ." He seemed to realize he was repeating himself again. "By the way, I'm Brian." He extended his hand toward her.

"I'm Carol." She shook his hand. "It was great seeing you too."

"Could I call you sometime? I mean, I'd love to thank you properly for helping me through an extremely tough time in my life. Let me buy you lunch." Realizing he was still holding her hand, Brian gently released it. "Sorry about that. I'd just like to see you again, I mean . . . as a thank-you."

"Well, I don't . . ."

"Please don't say no," he pleaded. "It would mean a lot to me. My life was a wreck when I met you, and you helped me begin to turn things around. I'm so grateful."

"I suppose lunch would be . . ."

"Great! I could call you in a day or so."

The sound of crashing waves jolted Carol from her flashback. She realized she had walked quite a distance on the beach and had lost all sense of time. She walked past a couple sitting on a towel, talking and touching as though they were in love. She wondered if they were married or if they were having an affair. They looked so happy, the way she and Carl had when they first got married.

On their first date, Carl had told her they were soul mates. And for the first seven years of their marriage, it seemed as if they were. They went everywhere and did everything together, and life was great. She found herself on occasion still trying to figure out what happened. Why had their marriage changed for the worse? At one point, she wondered if Carl was having an affair, but finding no evidence, she decided he was not. She cried and worried about why his affection had waned, but finally she just accepted it and decided to live with it. At least until Brian showed up.

Her thoughts turned back toward him. He didn't wait a day or so to call; he called that afternoon—and the next, and the next, and the next. His voice was so soothing on the phone that she looked forward to his calls. One lunch had turned into several lunches and then dinner at his place several times. Now Brian wanted more.

"I have a business trip scheduled next month. I'll be in Kansas City for three days. I'd like you to come with me," Brian had said.

"You know I can't do that."

"I've been thinking about this. You told me you have a girlfriend in Chicago. Couldn't you say you were going to visit her for a few days? Wouldn't she cover for you?"

"Brian, come on. Don't ask me to do this."

"Carol, you know how I feel about you, and I know you feel it too. We have something beautiful here; we need to see where it will lead us. From what you've told me, Carl is more of a housemate than a husband. You deserve to be happy, and I want to be the man who makes sure you are."

"I don't know."

"Am I right? Do you feel something happening between us?"

"Yes, of course I do, but—"

"Then come with me," Brian pleaded. "Give us a chance. You know it's just a matter of time before you're going to have to leave Carl. You're a beautiful young woman. You should have a man who loves and cares for you, a man who gives you the time, attention, and affection you deserve. Come with me."

"I'd have to get someone to look after Sarah. I guess I could ask my sister."

"Carl won't make a big deal over you going to visit a friend, right?"

"Right. He doesn't really care what I do. As long as Sarah is taken care of, he won't even question it."

"It's settled, then. I'll make our reservations and get our airline tickets."

The giggles of two little girls playing tag brought her attention back to the beach. It was starting to get dark, and her thoughts turned toward the long drive home, a hot shower, and a chance to talk with Brian before bed. She brushed the sand from her feet and slipped on the purple flip-flops. To assure that she was always prepared for a good relaxing walk on the beach, she'd been carrying a towel, blanket, and pair of flip-flops in the trunk of her car since her college days. The beach had become her place of solace, away from the marriage and husband who had once been her safe place.

When she walked in the house, seven-year-old Sarah greeted her. "Mommy, where have you been? Daddy's been looking for you."

"Hi, sweetie." She kissed the girl on her forehead.

"Can we have pizza for dinner? Dad said it's up to you. Please, Mommy, can we?"

"Yes, pizza is a good idea. Where's your dad?"

"He's in the kitchen, talking to a man."

"What man?"

"I don't know."

"Go upstairs, honey, and do your homework. I'll call you when the pizza is here."

"I already did my homework."

"Well, you can watch TV until the pizza comes, okay?"

"All right, but I'm really hungry for pizza. I think I can eat two whole pieces."

"Yes, baby, I'll order it in a few minutes. Just go upstairs."

The ache that had been in her stomach for several weeks was now a throbbing pain. Something was wrong. Carl seldom had visitors over to the house—and never without her knowing about it in advance. She walked into the kitchen slowly.

"Come on in," Carl said. He was seated at the table and there were two coffee cups, one in front of him . . . and one in front of Brian. "I invited a friend of yours over for coffee, and being the man he is, he accepted my invitation."

Carol stood in the doorway, unable to move. She looked over at Brian, whose eyes seemed to empathize with her. "But how did you . . . ?"

"He is a friend, right? After all, according to your cell phone, you talk several times a day, every day." Carl stood up and pulled out a chair at the table. "Sit, my dear sweet wife. Sit here between Brian and me."

"What are you doing, Carl?" she asked.

"Just trying to find out what my wife wants to do about our life together. I just want to know if this life we're living is a lie. I want to know why you are trying to ruin something we spent the last ten years building."

"Look, Carl, this is between me and you. Brian doesn't need to be here."

Carl's voice had started softly, but it began to escalate. "My dear wife, Brian does need to be here, because he says he's in love with you. And he says that the two of you are going away together next weekend. So I really think he needs to be here."

Carol had heard Carl raise his voice only once in the twelve years she'd known him, and that was before they were married and it wasn't directed toward her. She'd often said she had married the gentlest man she had ever known. In ten years of marriage, they never argued, and Carl never showed any signs of anger. Usually when they disagreed, Carl would say his piece and then surrender. Carol did not know this side of the man she married, and didn't think Carl was even capable of this kind of confrontation.

Brian spoke up. "I'm sorry, Carol. He asked me how I felt about you, and I told him. If I were in his shoes, I'd want to know the truth." Then Brian remembered he *had* been in Carl's shoes. It had been just three years prior that his ex had the affair that ended their six-year marriage. His whole life was turned upside down the day he learned of the affair. But he had learned the hard way, in the midst of lies that led to witnessing his ex's infidelity. The memory of that day sent a sick feeling through his stomach. It was an awful dé jà vu moment, except this time he was the other man.

Brian's tone changed. He began to speak in a soft, almost timid voice. "I mean, he . . . he deserves . . . A man deserves to know. A man deserves to know the truth." He could hardly force the words from his mouth. He remembered how much he loved his ex, who had been his childhood sweetheart. In his mind, her betrayal had nearly destroyed him. He was more familiar with what it felt like to be in Carl's shoes than he wanted to be.

"Yes, my dear wife," Carl said sarcastically. "The truth! You heard the man—I deserve it. If he were in my shoes, he'd want to know. So we both agree. The truth, Carol!"

"Carl, listen to me," Carol said. "We do need to talk, but not like this. If you want—"

Carl interrupted her, his voice even louder than before. "Just tell the truth. Are you planning to go away with him? Are you in love with him? Have you slept with him? What am I dealing with here? Just tell me!"

"We were planning . . . I mean, I was . . . I . . ." Carol paused and looked at Brian. "I'm confused. I don't know if—"

"What are you saying, Carol?" Brian interrupted. "Just tell him."

"I don't know what to say. I don't know about any of this. I need to . . . We—"

"Now that Carl knows about us, you're unsure?" Brian waited for Carol's response before continuing. "I thought you felt the same way that I do. Look, I know you didn't want him to find out this way, but there's no point in hiding it any longer. Tell him, Carol."

"It's just . . . It's just that I . . ." Carol stopped and held her head down.

Brian stood up. "This is our chance to be together. This could have been done a different way, but here it is—an opportunity I think we should take."

Carol was silent. Carl stared at her, his eyes burning into her core.

Brian started again, this time looking at Carl. "Listen, man, I'm sorry this thing came to you like this. But Carol and I—"

Carol interrupted. "Brian, I think you should leave. I need to talk to my husband alone."

"Your husband? Your *husband?* You've always referred to him as Carl. In all our conversations, you've never used the word 'husband.' But *now* you call him that? I find that interesting, Carol. Very interesting."

"Please don't make this any worse than it already is," Carol said, looking at Brian.

"So that's it? You want me to leave so you can talk to your *husband?*"

"Yes, please. Brian, just go. I'm sorry . . . but please just go," Carol pleaded.

Brian looked at Carl. "Thanks for the coffee, man." He started toward the door and then paused and looked back at Carol. She looked away to avoid seeing the hurt and disappointment on his face. Carl stood and walked Brian out of the kitchen. The front door slammed hard.

When Carl returned to the kitchen, he joined Carol at the table. They sat in silence for a long time. Their silence was interrupted when Sarah came bursting into the kitchen, full of energy.

"Where's the pizza, you guys? I'm hungry."

Sole Thoughts

So in everything, do to others what you would have them do to you . . .
MATTHEW 7:12 NIV

On any playground anywhere around the world, we could ask any children at play if they know the Golden Rule (or some version of it): "Treat others the way you want to be treated." Most likely, we would get an affirmative response. The Golden Rule is a tenet that's part of all the world's major religions. It is embedded in our various cultures and taught as a way of life in our educational systems and family settings. It is one of the most popular ideas we have related to improving relationships. And yet, like many of the moral and religious codes available to us, we, adults and children alike, falter as far as implementation. It is not so easy to practice this nice-sounding rule on a regular basis in every circumstance. Many would agree that when facing difficult situations, strong emotions can hijack one's reasoning ability.

It may help strengthen our effort to practice the Golden Rule if we understand how it works. Unless we've done some inner work, most of us miss that this rule has the ability, when practiced, to add meaning and value to our relationships as well as our overall peace of mind. The principle works like this: In relationships, if we treat others the way we would like them to treat us, we enact a great spiritual law—of sowing and reaping—in a positive way. We create high-quality relationships by sowing thoughts, words, and attitudes that are compassionate, kind, and caring. We will reap like benefits in return, although not necessarily from those with whom we have sown our good efforts. The unspoken wisdom behind the Golden Rule is that there is a link between what we think, say, and do toward others, and what others think, say, and do toward us.

One great challenge we all have, however, in practicing the Golden Rule is that we generally learn conduct from our experiences with others. For example, the child who is picked on while on the school playground may get the following counsel from the concerned parent: "The next time someone hits you, stand up for yourself. Hit the kid back." This may lead to a physical altercation for which there will be an excuse: "Well, Johnnie hit me first, so I hit him back." Before we realize it, our experiences can lead us to do to others *what they do* to us. And of course, we will still reap what we have sown, but the outcome may not be positive or harmonious.

Once we discover that there is great value in the thoughts, words, and actions we send out to others, we prepare ourselves to use good judgment in our interactions. Embracing the law of sowing and reaping gives us greater understanding to make a powerful choice on our own behalf, knowing that what we send out to others will come back to either haunt us or bless us.

As we examine how the Golden Rule works, there is another consideration: how we treat others reflects on some level what we believe about ourselves. If we are in the habit of treating others poorly, it's an indication that on some level, our self-esteem could use an upgrade. If we are in the habit of treating others well, it's a measure of higher self-esteem. Low or high, self-esteem can't help but show up in how we interact with others.

It is a demonstration of positive self-worth to enter into, and subsequently develop, connections with others that honor and support the best of who we are, and the best God created us to be. The more we practice the Golden Rule, the more we build character traits that promote inner well-being.

As we practice treating others the way we would like to be treated, we develop the character traits of empathy and fair-mindedness. Solomon prayed to God, *Give therefore thy servant an understanding heart to judge thy people, that I may discern between good and bad . . .* (1 Kings 3:9 KJV). The "understanding heart" is one filled with compassion and wisdom, two elements of the Golden Rule. When wisdom and love join forces, we draw on our ability to apply the solid judgment that comes from the Higher Self each of us has. This is the kind of judgment for which Solomon was remembered. It allows us to bypass our ego-centered assessments of the circumstances before us so that we may factor in compassion and divine guidance. Consistently doing so reveals that there is great value in treating others well.

In our interactions with others, if we can remember those simple words that came to Brian in his moment of revelation—"If I were in his shoes . . ."—we will begin a journey of compassion that is calibrated to increase our personal self-esteem and nourish our relationships. Most of us have heard this saying: "Walk a mile in someone else's shoes." In so doing, we may glimpse situations from their perspective, empathize with their position, and perhaps be more inclined to feel gentleness, humility, forgiveness, or acceptance.

When we make the effort to live by the Golden Rule, we are introduced to a pathway by which we may alter the way we cherish our connections with others and celebrate the peace of mind that naturally emerges from an understanding heart. In addition, the more we practice it, the more we heal from the pain that resulted when others, in their ignorance of this timeless formula, mistreated us the way someone mistreated them.

By its name, the Golden Rule tells us of a path to good fortune. Since ancient times, gold has been a symbol of wealth.

When Solomon asked God for an understanding heart, he exhibited the quality of character at the core of this rule—love and wisdom; Solomon was granted an understanding heart, good fortune, and vast material wealth. He is remembered as a wise king and one of the wealthiest men who ever lived. Gold is a valuable commodity to this day. The gold in the Golden Rule is found in the heart that understands that there are great rewards in the fair and compassionate treatment of others, and that true good fortune can be found in treating others the way we desire to be treated.

Extraordinary Step to Empower Your Sole's Journey

Let an understanding heart bless all your interactions with others.

If the Shoe Fits . . .

- Recall a specific instance when an understanding heart helped you resolve a relationship issue.
- Can you recall a past relationship that may have been improved if you had exercised the compassion to walk in someone else's shoes?
- Is there a current relationship that could benefit from a "shoe exchange," in which the two of you engage in some exercise that would allow you both to see from each other's point of view?

- When do you find it most difficult to apply the Golden Rule?
- What would be an Extraordinary Step toward expressing the compassion of an *understanding* heart in some relationship in your life right now?

8

Lucky Shoes

"Hey, Grandmommie, Grandmommie, look at me," the five-year-old boy called to the woman sitting on the park bench.

"I see you, Michael," the woman replied as she looked up from the book she was reading.

"Watch me. See how fast I can run."

Michael took off running as though he were competing against someone. As he ran, the little red lights in his shoes flashed like a neon billboard. With each movement, the lights seemed to give him added power that quickened his arrival at his destination—an oak tree. He slowed down just enough to tag the tree and quickly turn around for a new race with himself. On the return, he picked up speed and again the red lights flashed in perfect rhythm with each step. He ran back to the blue bicycle he had parked before he began demonstrating his racing skills.

"Did you see me, Grandmommie? Did you see me?"

"I did. You were wonderful! You're faster than you were the last time I was here."

"I know. I can run faster than Danny and Patrick."

"Who are they?"

"Two boys in my school. They can never catch me. I'm too fast for them."

"Do those shoes have anything to do with why you're so fast?" the woman asked with a smile.

"These are my lucky shoes, but I was fast even before my daddy bought them for me. I wear these when I race because I know I can win. I'm going to be winning a lot of races even when I get big."

"I believe you," the woman said with an even bigger smile. "God only knows how fast you'll be by the time I come back to visit next spring."

"Oh, I'll be very fast by then. I'm going to be a runner when I grow up, so I have to keep getting faster and faster." Without warning, young Michael took off running again.

"Grandma, Grandma, did you hear what I said?" asked Michael, now sixteen years old.

"I'm sorry, Michael. My mind wandered back in time."

"You must have been far, far away. I've been talking to you for the last few minutes, and you didn't even hear me."

"I was remembering one of our days in the park when you were little. You remember the park we used to go to when you lived on Bluff Lane?"

"Oh yeah. Winstead Park. You used to take me there to ride my bike whenever you visited us."

"I was just remembering a day when you were showing me how fast you could run. You had on shoes that had little red lights in them, and as you ran, the lights would flash like crazy."

"I remember that," Michael said. "I wish I had those shoes today. You know something, Grandma? I actually used to think those red lights in the shoes made me run faster."

"Well, it was like watching lightning in motion. It was a sight to behold," the woman said.

A voice came over the loudspeaker: "All runners please line up for the next race."

"This is it, Grandma. Wish me luck. I don't see my mom and dad. I hoped they'd make it here in time to see me race."

"Well, I'm sure they will be here as soon as they can. In the meantime, I'm here cheering for you."

"I'm wearing my new lucky shoes for this race. They don't have red lights in them, but they're my best, and I think I need all the help I can get today."

"What are you saying, Michael?"

"Well, it's just that the guys in this competition have already competed in this kind of race before, and this is my first time at this level. I have to come in at least third if I want to go to the state finals."

The woman took her grandson's hand. "Listen, when you were five, you told me you were fast before you got your lucky running shoes. Do you remember that?"

"Yes."

"You told me you wore them because you knew you could win. You had an attitude that was confident. Do you remember?"

"Yes, but I was just a kid. I didn't know how competitive these races would be."

"Michael, you told me you were going to be a runner. You told me you were going to be winning a lot of races." The woman paused to look her grandson directly in the eye. "You never said anything about third place. You've been preparing to be a first-place runner since you were five years old. No pair of shoes will be lucky for you if you don't have the will to give it everything you've got. So go out there, harness the will you have to win first place, and give it your best. I'll be right here watching the whole time, just like I said I would."

"You're right, Grandma, you're right." Michael turned and took off in a slow jog to line up for his race.

He returned not long after with a big smile on his face. "Grandma, did you see me? It was great! My fastest time so far!"

"Yes, yes, I saw the whole race. You were wonderful!"

"Did you see me on the takeoff? I took off like lightning."

"Just like with your old lucky shoes with the flashing red lights," the woman said with a big grin on her face.

"I guess these are my new lucky shoes," Michael said, looking down at his sneakers.

"I suppose you can say that as long as you remember that any luck you had was activated by your preparation and your will to stretch yourself. You won first place today because you were confident, and you were ready. And yes, good-quality shoes are important, but, my dear fast-running grandson," the woman said, pointing at the boy's chest, "you did the work."

"Grandma, I think you bring me luck. You've been at all my races this past year and I took first place every time."

"Yeah, so I'm like a lucky pair of shoes," the woman said with a chuckle.

"You're so funny." They both laughed and began walking toward the exit.

"I guess Mom and Dad didn't make it," Michael said as he looked around for his parents.

"Your mom called just before the race started. She said they got delayed getting out of work, but they will meet us at the restaurant to celebrate your taking first place."

"She said that before the race?" Michael asked. "She actually said I'd take first place?"

"Yes, she did."

"How could she know I'd take first place?"

"I told your parents when they called that you were going to win first place and that we'd need to celebrate afterward."

"You told them that? Suppose I . . . What if . . . ?"

"All these years you've been training for a far greater prize than a first-place ribbon or trophy. Your running has taught you that if you put your mind to something, focus your personal will on the task at hand, and follow through on the outer work, you have a formula to win a lot more than a race."

"What do you mean?"

"Michael, you may not always win first place, but if you believe in yourself and do your best, you can never lose. That goes for running and anything else you want to do in life." The woman took her grandson's hand. "And, my dear sweet grandson, you have the added gift of parents and a grandmother who love you, and who will believe in you no matter what—and that is your winning edge."

"I get it, Grandma, but if you don't mind, I'm still going to wear my lucky shoes whenever I race."

Sole Thoughts

Do you believe that I am able to do this?
MATTHEW 9:28

We all need believers in our lives, whether it's a grandparent, parent, sibling, spouse, child, or friend. There is no measure for the boost we gain in self-confidence when someone believes *in, for,* and *with* us, or the rewards we receive by doing the same for others.

When others believe the best on our behalf, if their motives are pure, if their overall consciousness is compassionate, and if they aspire to accept the wisdom God has embedded in all of us, they infuse us with "spiritual will." This personal will can be strengthened with hope, faith, and a strong desire to reach a worthy goal—that's when we demonstrate great potential. This is the quality of personal will addressed here.

Believers can lend us various levels of support. First, they believe *in* us. No matter what the circumstances, they want us to experience the best. They support us in whatever way they can so we can achieve what we desire. They see potential in us and inspire us to spend our energy living up to that potential. What they see is not just based on physical or mental ability. They see our deeper spiritual essence and believe in the power of God that's active within us.

Second, believers believe *for* us. If we get weary along the way, they are willing to carry the torch of triumph for us, even if we adopt self-defeating thoughts, words, and actions. They lend us their belief in our higher spiritual ability to help us cross the finish line. They see our setbacks as temporary. These believers do not doubt, for they know that with God, all things are possible.

Third, believers believe *with* us. They join their belief with ours, and together our believing power is magnified to the point of demonstrating personal will that is in tune with our highest good. This is the ideal state toward accomplishing our heart's desire. In this way, our personal will can be directed by God's guidance toward good results in every situation.

Believers have identifiable characteristics. They are exceptional in looking for the good in themselves, in others, and in circumstances. Most likely, they've had a few tough times themselves, and by the power of believing, they pulled through. Perhaps at some point along the way, someone believed in them and they felt strengthened by it. They do not underestimate the power of belief and know it is an effective tool toward the manifestation of hopes, dreams, and greater potential. They resonate with the words in the scripture. *Therefore I say to you, whatever things you ask when you pray, believe that you receive them, and you will have them* (Mark 11:24).

Believers know that when we believe with our whole hearts, a prayer goes out into the universe on our behalf. When two men came to Jesus asking to be healed, Jesus in turn asked them, "Do you believe that I am able to do this?" Only after they responded "Yes, Lord" did he respond positively to their request. By asking the question, Jesus caused the men to address their own beliefs and thereby activate their personal wills to be healed.

While it is extremely powerful having others believe in us, it is not a license to rely on luck or a substitute for believing in ourselves. When we subject ourselves to ongoing, self-infused, life-affirming injections of positive thoughts and self-talk, we build up our own inner believing power. With regular conversations with your Higher Self (some call this prayer), you can expect the unveiling of your true potential, and that your personal will be in alignment with God's will. Belief is the exclamation point on every prayer. In another healing parable, a man was fearful over his daughter's condition, and Jesus said to him, *Do not be afraid; only believe* (Mark 5:36).

Every moment we spend focusing on a positive outcome helps us move beyond our fears and strengthens our belief. Trust that God has given all of us the potential to succeed at many things. If we discover that we need to increase the belief in our own potential, the way to do it is to start believing in the positive potential of others. That's how belief works best—just do it. The more we exercise our power to believe in good, positive potential, the greater our capacity to experience a compelling will to succeed.

Luck, however, should not automatically be dismissed as a distracting trinket in which unearned hope is placed. Lucky shoes—or any other talisman by itself—will not bring us good fortune, success, fame, or happiness. Luck is an optimistic feeling that means we have great expectancy toward a favorable result. When we feel lucky, energy stirs within us. Perhaps we can't explain it, but it conveys a message: "A blessing is on the way!" Anytime our personal will is reinforced by our belief, strengthened by inner and outer preparation, we can't help but feel an elevated level of expectancy. Once we have prepared ourselves mentally, emotionally, physically, and spiritually, and have others around us who believe *in, for,* and *with* us, we have earned the right to anticipate a blessing and have every reason to own the attitude of expectancy that shows up as feeling lucky.

Extraordinary Step to Empower Your Sole's Journey

Activate personal spiritual will in those around you by believing *in, for,* and *with* them, allowing them to do the same for you.

If the Shoe Fits . . .

- Describe a time when you used your personal spiritual will toward manifesting something that required a strong belief in yourself.
- How would you explain what it means to feel lucky? Describe a situation where you ascribed luck to an object, person, set of circumstances, or pair of shoes?
- Can you think of someone who has demonstrated that they believe in you unconditionally? What effect has that had on you?
- Is there someone in your life who needs to know you believe in them? Who? Why?

- If you were surrounded by people who all believed *in, for,* and *with* you, what could you accomplish? How would you benefit? How would they benefit?
- What would be an Extraordinary Step for you toward the increase of your personal spiritual *will*?

9

Bloody Soles

THE KNOCK ON THE DOOR was loud and forceful.

"Mom," Shelly called to her mother. "There are two policemen at the door."

"Police?"

"Yeah," Shelly said. "Two of them."

The woman opened the door slowly. "May I help you?" she asked the officers.

"Good evening, ma'am. I'm Officer Williams, and this is Officer Brady. Are you the mother of Jake Anderson?"

"Yes."

"Jake Anderson lives here with you?"

"Yes. Yes, he does, Officer."

"Is he here now?"

"Yes, but what is this about?"

"We need to talk to your son, ma'am."

"But what's going on? Why do you need to talk to him?"

"Ma'am, we need to talk to your son. Now." Officer Williams moved in closer so he could see inside the house. "There's a party here tonight?"

"Yes, actually it's a party for my son. He's sixteen today."

The officer's tone was insistent. "Please, ma'am, get him now."

The woman turned to her fourteen-year-old daughter, who had been standing at the door the entire time. "Shelly, go get your brother and tell him to come quick."

Moments later Jake appeared. "Mom, what's going on?"

"Are you Jake Anderson?" Officer Williams asked.

"Yes, but what—"

The officer interrupted. "Please step outside so we can ask you a few questions."

"Why are you—" Jake's mother attempted to ask.

"Please, ma'am." Officer Williams held up his hand. "You can step outside with us too, but we need to talk to him."

The music from the basement stopped. Word spread that the police were outside questioning Jake on the front porch. Guests of the party started leaving the house by the back door.

"Do you know John Earl Baxter?" Officer Williams continued to probe.

"Yes," Jake replied.

From a larger paper bag, the officer pulled out a plastic bag that contained a pair of worn dress shoes. "Are these your shoes?"

Jake looked at them for a moment. "Yes . . . yeah . . . Those look like my shoes."

The officer turned the bag over to show the bottom of the shoes. "Whose blood is this on your shoes?"

"I don't know, Officer. I loaned those shoes to John Earl two days ago. How did you—"

"Why did you loan him your shoes?"

Nervously Jake explained, "Well . . . I . . . I invited him to my party, and he said he had no shoes to wear except his gym shoes, so I told him he could borrow an old pair of mine, but he never showed. We haven't seen him tonight."

"That's not the way John Earl tells the story," Officer Williams said.

Jake's mother interrupted. "What do you mean? What story? What did John Earl say?"

"Well, he was arrested tonight." Officer Williams paused, seeming to look for a reaction from Jake. "He said you were with him earlier and that the two of you broke into a house around the corner from here."

"No! No way he said that!" Jake said.

"Well, somebody's lying. There's blood on these shoes, and you admit they're yours."

"But how did you get them?" Jake asked. "I gave them to John Earl the day before yesterday, like I said."

"They were in his car when he was stopped earlier tonight. He was wearing gym shoes. These were on the floor on the passenger side. Did you leave them there when you got out?"

"I told you—I haven't seen John Earl since Thursday, and I don't know anything about a break-in."

"Well, son, I think we'd better go to the station. We're going to have to find out who's lying here."

"But I—"

"Listen, you admit that you know John Earl, you admit these are your shoes, and your shoes have blood on them. You'd better hope this blood doesn't match the victim's, or you're in a lot of trouble."

"What victim?" Jake's mother asked in a concerned voice.

"Mrs. Grayson. She lives on the next block in the corner house. It looks like she was assaulted by whoever broke in her house," the officer said as he looked at Jake.

Officer Brady stepped forward, grabbed Jake, and handcuffed him. "You have the right to remain silent . . ."

"Where are you taking him?" Jake's mother asked.

"You can meet us at the Twenty-Third Street station, ma'am."

"But I didn't do anything," Jake insisted as he looked at his mother and sister standing on the porch. "Mom, I swear. I didn't do anything."

The police car drove off. The few remaining teens who had been at the party had crowded around to see and hear what was going on. Jake's sixteenth birthday party was officially over, and no one could have predicted this kind of ending. Some of the guests lingered in the street talking about what had happened, and others slowly moved on until the front of the house was free of all Jake's friends. Except two girls.

As Jake's mother walked from the house toward her car, the two girls approached her. "Mrs. Anderson, I'm Karen Edwards, and this is Gwen Roberts. We go to school with Jake."

"It's nice to meet you girls, but this isn't a good time. I'm headed to the police station to find out what they're doing to my son."

"I know . . . We know," Gwen said. "That's why we waited to talk to you."

"Do you girls know something about this? Do you have some information that can help Jake?"

"Well," Karen said, "we don't know how much it will help, but . . ."

"What is it? If you know anything, please tell me."

"Everybody in school knew that John Earl was up to no good," Gwen said. "I mean, ever since he arrived here last year. I mean . . . everybody just knew he was into stuff that was . . . well, just wrong."

"We all tried to tell Jake," Karen said. "He wouldn't listen. He thought John Earl was his friend, but everybody knew . . . In fact, some of the others who were at the party tonight said that if John Earl turned up, they would just leave."

"What kind of stuff is John Earl into?" Jake's mother asked. "Would he do something like this?"

"We don't know, but he's bad news," Gwen said. "Jake was kind of gullible when it came to John Earl. He seemed to go along with whatever John Earl said. Jake is a good guy—everybody at school loves him; he genuinely cares about people. But . . . he had bad judgment getting involved with John Earl."

Karen added, "Yeah, I just hope—we all hope—that Jake comes out of this okay."

When Jake's mother arrived at the police station, she saw Officer Williams. "Where is my son?"

"He's being questioned, ma'am."

"When can I see him?"

"Just have a seat, Mrs. Anderson. If he doesn't confess, it's going to be a long night."

"Confess? He's not going to confess to something he didn't do. My son is innocent."

"I'm sure you believe that, ma'am," the officer said as he walked away.

After two hours of waiting, John Earl's parents arrived. "Mr. and Mrs. Baxter, I'm Eleanor Anderson, Jake's mother. I met you once at one of the basketball games."

"Yes, I remember," the woman said as her husband looked away.

"I don't know what's going on. They won't let me see my son," Jake's mother said.

"Well, our attorney will be here shortly," the man said. "We'll definitely be filing a suit for false arrest. Whatever your son is accused of has nothing to do with our son. He's not involved in this."

At that moment, the two women looked at each other, and a territorial coldness came between them. They had a revelation at the same time. They suddenly realized they both believed their sons were innocent, but one of them was most likely guilty of something—something that neither of them wanted to face. The women sat on opposite sides of the waiting room and never spoke to each other again.

A man wearing a dark blue suit walked into the waiting area. "Mrs. Anderson?"

"Yes." Jake's mother sprang to her feet. "I'm Mrs. Anderson. Where is my son? Can I see him? Is he all right?"

"Ma'am, please come this way." He led her down a long hallway without saying a word. He stopped and opened a door to a small room. "Have a seat." He motioned for her to sit opposite him at a wooden table. "I'm Detective James." He tossed a file folder on the table. "I have a problem," he said.

"What do you mean? Please tell me what's going on. No one will talk to me about my son. Please, Detective, I know my son is not involved in this."

"Actually, I believe you. I don't think your son had anything to do with this robbery that went terribly wrong."

"Then let him go," Jake's mother pleaded.

"It's not that easy, ma'am. We have a witness who saw John Earl outside the victim's house near the time the crime was committed."

"But what does that have to do with my son?"

"Well, John Earl is claiming that your son not only engineered the robbery, but that he was with him during the break-in. He says that when the victim walked in on them, Jake is the one who picked up the lamp and hit Mrs. Grayson. When we arrived, we found her unconscious and the lamp was near her body."

"Oh my God, Jake would never do that! That poor woman. We've known Mrs. Grayson for many years. Jake cuts her lawn sometimes and shovels her snow. He's known her since he was seven or eight. She always paid him well. Sometimes when he did an exceptional job, she would go back in the house and come out with a big tip. She gave him big bonuses for Christmas and on his birthdays too. She would send a bag of apples from her yard to me when Jake went to cut her lawn. He had no reason to do this to Mrs. Grayson."

"Well, according to John Earl, it was Jake's idea to rob her because he knew she kept money in the house. And you just admitted that Jake knew she kept money in the house."

"Yes, he knew, but that doesn't mean he did this." The woman shook her head. "I told my son last year when John Earl joined the basketball team that he was trouble. Something about him just didn't sit well with me. And tonight I learned from two girls who came to Jake's party that . . . well, I wasn't the only one who had suspicions about John Earl."

"Go on," Detective James said. "If you have any information that can help your son, this is the time to tell it."

"Just before I left the house to come here, two girls who go to school with Jake and John Earl said that everyone in school knew that John Earl was bad news. But my Jake always wants to befriend everybody; it's like his personal mission in life or something. He's been like that since he was a toddler—he would just walk up to perfect strangers and . . ." she paused for a moment to collect herself. "Anyway, these two girls said that John Earl might be capable of doing something like this."

"Well, Mrs. Anderson, your instincts were right, and the girls may be right as well. John Earl has quite a record for a seventeen-year-old. He was in trouble in Chicago before he and his parents moved here last year." Detective James looked through some of the papers in the file in front of him and then closed the folder. "Here's the bottom line. Unless I have a solid alibi for your son's whereabouts between four and six p.m., there's not much I can do about John Earl's statement. I think he's trouble, but I have to work with the evidence. The shoes belong to your son, and we feel certain the blood on them will prove to be the victim's."

"Oh my God." Jake's mother buried her face in her hands for a moment. "This can't be happening. Today is my son's sixteenth birthday. I've been planning his party for three months. He's a good boy, Detective. I know my son. He loves life and people too much to ever hurt anyone. He couldn't have done this horrible thing to Mrs. Grayson."

"I'm going to need you to tell me every detail you can think of about where he was today. Your son is in a lot of trouble here."

"I sent Jake to the store around three thirty this afternoon to get cheese and butter for the macaroni and cheese I was making for his party."

"Are you sure about the time?" Detective James asked.

"Yes, I'm sure. Shelly, my daughter, had just come in from her dance class, and I looked at the clock. It was three twenty-five. I was about to send her to the grocery store for what I needed, but Jake said he would go because he had to stop at the barber shop to get his hair cut."

"How far is the barber shop from your house?"

"It's two blocks."

"What about the grocery store? How far is it from the barber shop?"

"It's three or four blocks."

"Do you know about what time it was when Jake returned?"

"It was just after five."

"Are you sure?"

"Yes. My TV show had just ended, and Jake walked in shortly after that."

"That's basically the story Jake told us. However, there was still time for him to meet up with John Earl, break in the house, commit this crime, leave his bloody shoes in the car, and return home just after five. Do you see why I have a problem here? The timing of Jake's story doesn't give him a sufficient alibi. Of course we'll check with the barber, and the grocery story, but there is still a small window of time that may leave suspicion."

There was a knock on the door, and Officer Williams stuck his head in the room. "Detective, may I see you for just a moment?" The two men talked outside for a few minutes.

Detective James returned to the room to say, "Mrs. Anderson, another witness just came forward and stated that when John Earl left Mrs. Grayson's house, he was alone, and there was no one with him when he drove off. Apparently, when the officer told John Earl that we had two witnesses, he changed his story and made a full confession. He admitted your son was not with him. We'll be releasing Jake, and you can take him home."

"Praise God!" The woman buried her face in her hands for a moment. "Thank you, God!"

"You can go back to the waiting room. We'll be bringing your son out in a few minutes."

"Thank you, Detective. Thank you so much."

As she walked back to the waiting room, she saw John Earl's parents in one of the other interrogation rooms. His mother was crying, and his father seemed to be arguing with Officer Williams.

"Ma" Jake ran toward his mother.

"Jake!" Mother and son embraced for a moment in silence.

"Mom, I was so scared. They tried to make me say I was with John Earl and that I hit old lady Grayson."

"Are you okay?"

"Yeah, I'm all right. I just can't believe John Earl would do something like this. Old lady Grayson has always been nice to me. I just can't believe it."

"I know, son, I know."

"I don't understand why John Earl would do this and try to put it on *me*. I was the only friend he had. No one else in school would even talk to him."

"Jake, two girls from school, Karen and Gwen, said that everybody in school knew John Earl was trouble and tried to warn you. Is that true?"

"Yeah, but John Earl didn't make friends easily. I thought that eventually people would like him if they saw that he was my friend. I don't think that . . . Well, I didn't think that John Earl was so bad, not like everybody thought."

"Did you have any idea that John Earl has a police record? Did you know he was involved in . . . God knows what?"

"A few times he said some things that . . . Well, I didn't think he was serious about the stuff he was talking about. I thought it was just talk."

"Jake, what were you thinking?"

"I don't know, Mom. I . . . I had no idea he would go through with it."

"I knew there was something about him the first time you brought him to the house, the day he joined the basketball team. Something about him didn't feel right. I should have done something."

"What do you think is going to happen to him? His dad is some kind of big shot, and John Earl always said his father can fix anything."

"Jake, this is a serious crime. Mrs. Grayson is in the hospital fighting for her life, and John Earl confessed. He's in a lot of trouble; there's no way to fix this. I hope you realize that you were almost pulled into this with him. I know you always want to help people, but this time . . ."

"You know something, Mom?" Jake was thoughtful for a moment. "I've got to believe that John Earl would have eventually told the truth, even without the second witness. I mean, I really thought we were friends. I knew he had some problems, but I thought I could help by being a friend. I'm so sad about what happened to Mrs. Grayson; I hope she'll be okay. But I don't think John Earl went there to do anything other than get some money from her. I think that . . ."

Detective James quickly approached with a clipboard and a pen. "Mrs. Anderson, I just need you to sign here. We'll need to keep Jake's shoes as evidence. I don't suspect he'd want them back anyway."

"No, sir," Jake said. "I never want to see those shoes again."

"Young man," Detective James said, "from now on, I suggest you select your friends with a lot more care. Like it or not, these bloody shoes belong to you. If John Earl hadn't confessed, I'd be holding you in this case—and not just your shoes. I hope that from this day forward young man, you will watch your step."

Sole Thoughts

Even my own familiar friend in whom I trusted,
Who ate my bread, Has lifted up his heel against me.
PSALM 41:9

Blood represents our life force. If we find blood on the bottom of our shoes, perhaps we made a misstep; a wrong, unwise choice; or went down a life-threatening path. And if a friend is the cause of the blood on our shoes, it could be that the misstep was in the selection of that friend and the maintenance of that connection.

Most of us know what it feels like to be betrayed by someone close to us. We ask ourselves how we could have trusted that person. It can be difficult to understand the reasons why good friendships go bad and the reasons that good intentions in relationships are sometimes one-sided. Sometimes we interrogate ourselves: "Why didn't I see this coming?" or "How could I have been such a poor judge of character?" These may be appropriate questions when we discover that betrayal and deceit have entered a relationship.

Relationships are so important to our overall happiness and well-being that mindful selection of friends and associates is an important life lesson we must all learn. If we find that we've been betrayed more than a few times by those we thought we could trust, we should reevaluate how we select the people with whom we spend time and do business. While we certainly do not want to make a habit of viewing our relationships from a suspicious standpoint, neither do we want the blood of another on the soles of our shoes or on the soul of our conscience.

And what of the one who is driven to betray another? To what or whom is he or she disloyal? When we use our own life energy to do harm to another, we betray ourselves. We waste our life energy in many ways, from living self-destructively to not using the talents God has given us to misusing our mental and emotional strength in an attempt to embezzle blessings that belong to another. We betray our own potential by allowing negative mental and emotional influences to take up residence in our consciousnesses until the flow of life's potency is clouded and weakened.

We all know the importance of having our heart pump clean, unencumbered blood through our veins. The heart represents the center of love, and it's crucial for life-supporting blood to keep the body in good health. The betrayer damages his own heart, and his own love for life is compromised. The betrayer disrupts the flow of power that supports the full expression of life. Erroneous thoughts, words, and actions become a sentence of personal and sometimes literal imprisonment. The betrayer faces punishment for the consequences of a weakened life force, which allowed him to succumb to the worst instead of God's best.

God has endowed us with inner and outer life. The inner life is directed by our thoughts. When our thoughts are life affirming, we honor the very blood that flows through our veins as the energy and vibration of God. The outer life is shaped by the quality of thoughts we entertain on the inner level. Aware of the connection between our inner and outer experience, we are challenged to think about ourselves and those around us in a manner that portrays respect for life. We owe it to ourselves to be equally vigilant over the selection of friends and associates, realizing that their inner life will affect the outer life we share together. In subtle and not-so-subtle ways, the people we regularly spend time with influence the experiences we have. We are all guilty by association; it's just a matter of *what* we're guilty of. Friendships built on a foundation of similar character traits, values, goals, and common interests go a long way toward creating high quality connections. However, a mutual respect for life and how one uses his or her life energy can also be important criteria for building healthy relations. We add to the quality of our own lives when we engage in relations that add vibrant, uplifting energy to our lives.

In many relationships that have included betrayal and dishonesty, there were often early warning signs. Perhaps we were too close to the situation and totally missed a little lie here or a little lie there. Perhaps we misread a carefully crafted story as an awkward statement or idle use of words. But the signs are usually there long before trouble hits.

Suspicions can be quickly dispelled or avoided altogether if we are alert and attentive to those we are connected to. Thoughtful listening is a loving thing to do, and it can be helpful in establishing healthy relationships. The more we develop and express our love for life, the more we use that love to help influence the choices we make regarding whom we spend time with.

But even with careful, mindful selection of friends and associates, we may still find ourselves facing emotional cuts and wounds. When trouble arises in a relationship, there are two main strategies for resolution: stay or walk away. Life supplies an abundance of opportunities for us to grow, so either choice has the potential to stretch us. The test of true friendship is in the ability of the parties involved to grow beyond the hurts, disappointments, and betrayals that sometimes find their way into relationships. The good news is, just like the blood we shed from a cut on our skin, emotional wounds can also heal if we are willing to allow it. The choice to stay is to accept the challenge and opportunity of forgiveness.

However, there are times when we need to walk away. It could be a safety issue, legal issue, moral issue, or it's simply time to move on. Walking away does not necessarily mean running away from issues we need to face; sometimes it is simply in our best interest (and theirs also) to end a friendship or association. Sometimes we see it clearly, and other times we will need to be open to the wise counsel of others who may be able to see for us what we have not been able to detect for ourselves. If we have solid relations with others around us, there may be occasions when we can benefit from their input. Listening to good advice from someone who has our best interests at heart can be another positive way to honor and respect the quality of life we choose to live.

Extraordinary Step to Empower Your Sole's Journey

Choose friends and associates whose honor and respect for life—their own and others'—is compatible with yours.

If the Shoe Fits . . .

- In what ways do you demonstrate your personal respect for life—yours and the lives of others?
- Have you ever felt betrayed by a friend? Looking back, can you recall any early signs of a problem? Why did you ignore them?
- Have you ever been accused of betraying someone? What did you learn from the experience?
- Have you ever worn shoes that you knew would hurt your feet by the end of the day? If so, why did you wear them? If not, why is this not an issue for you?
- Can you identify ways that you may have betrayed yourself?
- What qualities of character do you seek in your relationships with friends, associates, or with an intimate partner? Are there differences? Explain.
- What would be an Extraordinary Step you could take right now that would demonstrate greater honor, respect, and appreciation for your own *life*?

10

Broken Heel

THE PLANE RIDE HAD BEEN bumpy, and the turbulence mirrored her emotional state. But when she walked into the hotel lobby, its beauty allowed her, just for a moment, to set aside all the thoughts she wanted desperately to escape. It was the perfect place for her personal retreat, a carefully planned and private getaway.

The hotel sat directly in front of the beach. There was a luxury spa as well as four restaurants catering to different tastes, desires, and moods. A few blocks away was a shopping district. From the looks of the lobby, it was all that the brochure said it would be, and a good place for the kind of therapy Daena hoped would help solve her dilemma.

"Checking in, ma'am?"

"Yes. I have a reservation for five days of peace and contemplation. I've already turned my cell phone off."

The young man behind the counter chuckled at her enthusiasm. "May I have your picture ID?"

He took her driver's license and typed her name in the computer. "Okay, Ms. Fredrick, we have you down for five days in the Queen's Suite—king-size bed and an ocean view. And your room is ready."

"Ahh." Daena released a deep breath. "A suite with an ocean view— exactly what I need. Thank you." *Yes, time alone to think. I'm about to make either one of the best decisions of my life or one of the worst mistakes in twenty years.*

"You have an all-inclusive package, so all you'll need to do is show this card at any of the restaurants on the property for your meals, and for your daily access to the spa. Here is another card for drinks in the bar, and there is no limit on the drinks."

"Oh my! I don't think I'll need this." She carefully placed the second card back on the counter. "I hope I won't resort to drinking my way through my retreat."

The young man smiled as he slid the card back to her. "Well, just hold on to it. I have to make sure that I give our guests everything on our quality assurance checklist."

"Okay. I seldom drink, but hey, I am staying in a luxury resort. I just might decide to indulge in a glass of wine." Daena took the card from the counter. "In fact, that might be exactly what I need."

Still smiling and nodding his head in agreement, the man said, "Enjoy your stay, Ms. Fredrick." He handed her a key. "I'll have your bags delivered to your room." As she turned to walk away, he said with a chuckle, "Oh, just in case you do decide to have that glass of wine, the bar is open until three a.m."

On the elevator ride up to the seventh floor, Daena had plenty of time to think about Jay. "I need time to think," she had told him repeatedly over the previous two weeks. *Why couldn't things just stay the way they were? Any other time, talking would be fine, but not now, and not about . . .*

"Wow," she said as she opened the door to her suite. It was like a picture from an interior design magazine, and yes, the view of the ocean was breathtaking. She had paid a healthy sum for the suite, yet she had no regrets. *I'm worth it, I deserve it, and right now I need it. With both my kids off to college on full scholarships, this is my time to enjoy the life I've put off for too long.*

The knock at the door startled her. "I have your baggage, ma'am."

"Yes, thank you."

The young man placed two pieces of luggage carefully near the spacious closet. She handed him a generous tip.

"Thank you, ma'am. Enjoy your stay. If you need anything, just call the front desk."

Alone at last in her suite, she dove into the smaller of the two bags. She pulled out a five-by-seven picture frame and stared at the picture. Just before she left Chicago, Jay had given her a picture of himself and his girls. "Just remember, I love you, and in time the girls will grow to love you, too," he had said. He thought those words would comfort her, but they did not. They did just the opposite.

A full-body eighty-minute massage was first on her agenda. The relaxation she hoped for was slow to kick in. It was as if Jay's spirit were in the room, and she couldn't avoid her thoughts. When she turned forty, she had made a decision to put her needs and desires first. It had taken two failed marriages and raising two kids mostly on her own, and she didn't want to turn back. Now at forty-two, a wonderful man who was six years younger threatened the freedom she had just begun to appreciate.

"Ms. Fredrick, I'll step out of the room so you can get dressed. Would you like some water?"

"Yes, please."

Daena dressed slowly. When the masseuse came back into the tranquil space, she handed Daena a cup of water, which she downed immediately.

"Would you like more?"

"Yes. I'm thirsty and feel a bit light-headed."

"That happens sometimes. Let me get you more water. Just sit here until I get back."

The masseuse returned carrying two cups. "You're dehydrated. Haven't you been drinking water lately?" She handed Daena one of the cups.

"I guess I haven't." She drank the water and reached for the other cup.

"Your muscles were very tense. Is everything okay?"

"I'm going to be making a big decision in my life. That's why I'm here—to have some time alone to think."

"Well, there's still a lot of tension in your body. You know, feeling stress and worry isn't the best way to make a decision. Why don't you lie down for a few more minutes? I don't have another client for twenty minutes so try to relax."

Later that night, Daena could not get any restful sleep. Day two and three were much the same. There were more massages, a dip in the swimming pool, meditation, a long walk on the beach, journaling, reflection, and several late night glasses of wine, but still no decision.

On day four, Daena woke knowing it would be the last full day of her retreat. *I can't go back without a decision. Jay will want to know my answer, and I need to tell him something.* She pulled out a small notebook she had used as a journal for this trip. She read the entry from the day before:

> *I feel small and shallow when I think of walking away from a good man because I don't want to be a mother to his three girls. I just don't see myself raising young children again. Why? What's wrong with me? Why can't I just do it? I've raised my two kids, and I'm a good mother to them, so why is this so difficult for me? They're good little girls—four, seven, and nine. If I hadn't already raised my kids, who knows? I might feel differently. I enjoy being with them sometimes. Before Jay's ex decided she didn't want the girls to live with her, things were great. When we talked of marriage then, it was different. He had the girls every other weekend, and I was able to manage that. Sometimes I'd hang out with them and other times not. I had a choice. I had a choice. I had a choice.*

Daena turned to a clean page and stared at it for a few minutes before she began to write:

> *Even if I thought I could take on being a stepmother to three little girls, I don't think I can deal with the drama that Jay's ex is sure to bring. She says she doesn't want the girls now, but who's to say a year from now, or two or*

three, just when we're all adjusted, she won't want them back? I just don't want that confusion in my life. I did that whole drama thing over the children with my two exes, and I just don't see that for myself again. I don't want to go back to those painful times I've already survived. But Jay is a wonderful man. I do love him, but is that enough? Is the love in my heart enough to overcome all the doubt, fear, and worry rushing through my head? I don't know. I just don't know.

Dear God, I need some kind of sign so I'll know what to do and have the courage to do it. Please hear my prayer. I need help.

She closed the journal and started talking aloud to herself. "Shopping! That's what I need. I'll get dressed and go shopping. I always feel better when I shop." She looked in the closet. "Yellow—that's good. Bright colors will cheer me up, and yellow is the color of illumination, decision, and confidence."

Daena decided on a pair of pink open-toed shoes with three-inch heels, a pink-and-yellow top, and a pair of yellow capri pants. After getting dressed, she took the picture of Jay and the girls from the nightstand and stared at it for a moment. She said one last silent prayer: *Dear God, what should I do? Please give me some kind of sign.* She put the picture frame in her large purse and took off for the lobby.

"Just walk three blocks to your left and you'll see all the shopping you can stand," said the concierge, who directed her to a place called Shoppers Village. It was a touristy area with street vendors, boutiques, restaurants, souvenir shops, and jewelry stores.

"Do you need any help?" a saleswoman asked as Daena attempted to force herself into a shopping mood.

"Yes, I'll take these." Daena handed her two T-shirts, one for each of her children. *If I were married to Jay, I'd be buying five T-shirts.*

"Will that be all?"

"Yes, just the two T-shirts. Just two."

Moving slowly from store to store, Daena spent a lot of time looking but bought very little. This was the first time in a long time that her heart was not really into shopping. Every outfit and every piece of jewelry she looked at, she wondered if Jay would like it on her. But then she would think of his girls, and guilt would set in. *The girls deserve a stepmother who wants to be a mother to them, especially since their own is giving them up. How could Debbie give up her kids? The girls will need the assurance that they are loved. I just don't know if I can do it.*

After three hours, all she had purchased were the two T-shirts, a pair of earrings, and a pair of flat brown sandals. Shopping had not filled the void or revealed anything resembling an answer. It was time to return to the hotel, and Daena felt empty. No answer. No sign. No decision.

On the walk back, Daena thought about the day when what she thought was a perfectly good relationship had changed.

"We need to talk about something." Jay had motioned for her to sit next to him on the sofa.

"This sounds serious," she remembered saying.

"Well," he said, "it is." He took her hand in his. "Debbie called. She wants me to take the girls."

"Take them where? What do you mean?"

"She met some guy and says she's going to move to Seattle to be with him. She doesn't want to take the girls. She wants me to take them."

"For how long?"

"Indefinitely. She says she's going to marry the guy. Apparently, he travels a lot, and she wants to be free to travel with him. I told her I would only take them if she gives me full legal custody, and she agreed."

"Wow, that's quite a blow. Do the girls know?"

"Not yet. I wanted to talk to you first."

"How could Debbie give up her girls? I don't know what to say."

"Look, I know this is not how we planned things for us, but we've been talking about getting married, and we know we love each other, so I was just thinking we could make all this work together."

"Jay, honey, what are you saying?"

"Let's get married. I know we talked about next year, but we love each other, right? Let's just get married now."

"Because you'll have the girls, you want to get married now?"

"Daena, you know I don't mean it like that. You know I love you. I'm just asking if we should move our time frame up. There are going to be adjustments, and I thought we could make them all at once . . . and all together."

"I need time to think about this." Daena removed her hand from his. "This is a big decision. We talked about me starting my business and—"

"You'll still be able to do that. We'll—"

"You and I talked about traveling, and doing some of the things we both said we want to do. With Greg and Casey in college and you only having the girls every other weekend . . ."

"I know, I know. We'll still do all the things we've talked about. We'll just have to put some things off for a few years," Jay said.

"A few years? *A few years?* Jay, do you hear yourself? Kayla is four. You're talking about when she finishes school, and she hasn't even started kindergarten yet. Niki is seven and so racked with fear of abandonment that she still pees her bed. And Lilly, at nine years old, is so starved for attention that she's already trying to get boys to notice her. These girls need a lot. They need dedicated time and attention from a mother and a father." Daena rose to her feet. "I just don't know . . ."

Jay stood up and attempted to take her hand, but she pulled away. "Daena, listen to me. I'm sorry for putting you through all this now. It is a lot to ask. But we can work through all this. Maybe we could get your business going in a few years when Kayla is in school all day and—"

"Just stop, Jay. Stop. I need time to think about all this. This is a lot to absorb at one time."

The sound of traffic on the narrow side street brought Daena back to her walk from Shoppers Village. All of a sudden, her heel got caught in a crack in the sidewalk. Before she knew it, she was on the ground—but not on the sidewalk; she had fallen into the street. She looked up to see a car headed toward her. In a split second, a thought flashed: *I cannot die. Jay deserves the truth.*

The oncoming car stopped. A woman got out and ran to Daena as she lay in the street. "Oh my God, are you all right? Are you okay?"

"I think so," Daena said.

"I'm sorry. I . . . I'm so sorry."

A couple who had been walking behind Daena rushed over.

"Can you stand?" the man asked. He took one arm, and the woman who was with him took Daena's other arm.

"I think so. I don't think anything is broken," Daena said.

The couple lifted Daena to her feet and escorted her to the sidewalk. The driver of the car picked up the two shopping bags and Daena's purse, plus the few items that had fallen out of it.

"Oh, I'm so sorry. It looks like your picture frame is cracked," the driver said.

"Please just place it in my purse," Daena said. "Thanks." The picture of Jay and his three girls was cracked straight down the middle.

"That's not all that's broken," the man said. He pointed to the heel of Daena's shoe, still stuck in the crack in the sidewalk.

Daena looked down to confirm that the heel had indeed separated completely from the body of the shoe.

"How do you feel?" the man asked.

"I'm okay. I think I can stand on my own. Thank you."

The driver handed Daena her two shopping bags and purse. "I'm glad you're okay and grateful I wasn't speeding. If you're sure you're all right, I'll take off."

"I'm fine. Really."

The woman turned and went back to her car.

The man pulled the broken heel from the crack and handed it to Daena. "I guess you won't be wearing these again."

The couple turned and resumed their walk as Daena said one last thank you.

She reached into one of her bags, pulled out the pair of sandals she had purchased, and put them on. She threw the pink shoes in the bag, broken heel and all. "I'm fine," she said to herself. "I'm fine."

She walked back to the hotel slowly, partly because her right leg felt a bit of pain from the fall and partly because she was shaken by the experience. She said a prayer of gratitude. She acknowledged that the fall could have been worse, even fatal. And then she remembered what had flashed in her mind while she was lying in the street looking at the oncoming car.

When she walked into her suite, she went straight to the trash can. She pulled the broken picture frame from her purse, carefully removed the photo, and tossed the frame. She suddenly realized that she no longer felt anxious. She had her answer. She felt like her old self again, unburdened of the weight of being forced into a decision. She knew what to do.

Daena reached into her shopping bag and pulled out the pink shoes. She took a long pause, a deep breath, and then said aloud, "Sometimes God answers prayers in strange ways." She dropped the shoes in the trash, tossing in the broken heel last.

Sole Thoughts

Others, testing Him, sought from Him a sign from heaven.
LUKE 11:16

Unlike the crowd who gathered around Jesus to test the authenticity of his connection with God, many of us request a sign from God to clarify, confirm, or gain greater understanding of our own ability to preside wisely over our own affairs. There are times when we yearn to glimpse the unseen hand of God, giving helpful clues to solve the dilemmas we face. The solution could be as simple as right or left, stop or go, wait or move forward slowly. Perhaps the fog of confusion has obstructed our view of the guidance that seems just beyond reach, or maybe we lack the courage to act on a tough decision. Our prayer is for divine assurance of the direction that is best, an alternative that we may not have considered or simply the confidence to fearlessly leap into action.

However, you may want to take into consideration a few things before asking for a sign from God. The old saying "Be careful what you pray for because you just might get it" applies to this idea. The sign you receive may indeed present you with the clarity you seek, but the answer may not be what you hoped for. If this is the case, you may have a new predicament in having to decide to accept or deny the response. So before asking for a sign, ask yourself, "Am I really open to receive God's response?"

In addition, *how* the sign is delivered may be peculiar to your human comprehension of the situation. God expresses in and through you as your Higher Self, so whatever sign you receive will include you as a full participant in the response, even if what occurs seems bizarre or elaborate. To ask for a sign is to commission your Higher Self to orchestrate the unexpected, and yes, sometimes the very dramatic. Another question you might consider is this: "Am I willing to cooperate with whatever presentation my Higher Self will craft to draw forth the clarity I seek?"

The level of audacity in God's response will depend on your state of mind. Sometimes we're so consumed by a challenge that we have difficulty recognizing God's reply, so bold methods are applied to get our attention. This brings us to another question you might consider: "What measures must I take to keep my mind at peace and ready to receive God's answer?" A confused, worried state of mind may delay the clarity you seek.

Asking for a sign is simply another form of stating a prayer request. The question is more about confirming the extent of your faith in the power of prayer. Your response to these and other self-inquiries can make all the difference in your ability to gain the clarity, understanding, and confirmation you need to move forward.

In our story, Daena asked for a sign, and she received it. What she did not consciously know is that the answer would come at a moment when she was looking into oncoming traffic as she lay in the street fearing for her life. The near-fatal accident definitely got her attention. The cracked picture frame highlighted the object of her concern. The answer emerged from her Higher Self: tell the truth. It's so simple that if we didn't already know she was stuck in confusion, we might wonder why she didn't realize the answer before all the drama. But the broken heel helped make it clear. A broken heel will slow us down, cause us to move forward with greater caution, or make us stop in our tracks. Daena did all the things she knew to get her answer. She gave herself a personal retreat, wrote in her journal, got a massage, meditated—all good things to do. But her moment of clarity came when her mind was completely void of her dilemma. The broken heel caused her to forget about her challenge for a moment—that's when the answer came through clearly. A pause from worry can be just enough time for the Higher Self to reveal the guidance we seek.

One way we can enhance our receptivity to the guidance we seek is to temporarily separate ourselves from our daily distractions or from the people who may influence the situation we're praying about. This is a great time to employ all the spiritual practices we know. In some instances a change in venue alone can facilitate a mental shift away from worry and doubt, leading us toward hope and faith. Anything we can do to draw on greater faith will help deliver us to a state of consciousness where wise decisions are unveiled.

When we ask God for help, we set our faith in motion. Faith is the inner work we do to proceed in the assurance that our prayers will be answered. An earnest prayer is a pronouncement from the deeper levels of one's being. It signals intention to receive the guidance we seek. When we ask for a sign from this state of consciousness, we affirm that God does indeed answer prayer, and that we want God's response to our particular concerns, no matter how it is revealed. With our faith intact, we are ready to accept our highest good. And then, in God's wondrous and sometimes mysterious way, our answers are revealed through whatever methods and attention getters are available—even if it's through a near-fatal accident, a cracked picture frame, and a broken heel.

Extraordinary Step to Empower Your Sole's Journey

Stand firm in your faith that God answers prayers, even if the answers come in unexpected circumstances or unusual methods. Stay open to the many possibilities of how the answer will be revealed.

If the Shoe Fits . . .

- What part has your faith played in receiving answers to your prayers?
- Did you ever pray for a sign to be revealed to you? If so, what sign did you receive? If you've never prayed for a sign, why not?
- Can you think of an unusual or unsuspecting way that a prayer was answered for you or someone you know?
- When you are seeking guidance in any area of your life, what is your process? If the guidance appears delayed, what do you do next?
- When did you last go on a personal retreat? When is your next one?
- Have you ever been faced with a decision that caused you to avoid speaking the truth? Why did you hesitate?
- Have you ever had a pair of shoes malfunction in some way while you were wearing them? What did you think of it at the time? What do you think about it now?
- What would be an Extraordinary Step toward the demonstration of greater *faith* in your life right now?

11

Bowling Shoes

"Take your shoes off."

"Why?"

"That's how it's done. When the man comes over here, we tell him what size shoes we want. He gives us bowling shoes."

"Why can't I just wear my own shoes?"

"Street shoes will mess up the lanes. Now take your shoes off."

"Hey, Eli, what's up?" said a tall thin man who appeared behind the counter.

"Just introducing my little brother to the game."

"Didn't know you had a little brother," the man replied.

"Yeah, this is my brother, Nat. He needs a size seven . . . and a size ten for me."

"I don't wear no seven," Nat said. "I wear size eight."

"Your brother has big feet."

"Yeah, we tease him a lot at home. He's pretty big for an eight-year-old."

"You won't be able to call him your little brother for long." The man laughed as he plopped two pairs of rough-looking shoes on the counter. "Fifty cents," he said.

"We have to pay for these beat-up shoes?" Nat protested.

Eli put fifty cents on the counter and turned to his little brother. "Just put the shoes on, and stop complaining. You've got a lot to learn."

"It just seems like . . . well, if you're serious about the game," Nat said, "you should wear some decent shoes instead of these old—"

Eli interrupted. "Boy, you don't even know if you're serious about bowling. It's your first day, so shut up and come on."

Over the next three years, Eli proceeded to instruct his brother on the ways of bowling. They bowled on weekends during the school year and three to four times a week in the summer months. After Eli left for the army, Nat continued to bowl. Some of the older guys at the bowling alley took an interest in him. It was often said that Nat had what it took to go pro. By age nineteen, he was playing in tournaments with guys twice his age, and he was more than able to make a good living at bowling. Over the years, his skills grew, and he developed a focused passion for winning. Some say that was his downfall.

By age twenty-seven, Nat had won enough tournaments to have his own philosophy about winning: "When you look good, practice your behind off, and have a positive attitude when you walk on the lane, winning is inevitable." He lived his three-step winning philosophy and it proved to work for him. The problem was that bowling is a team sport.

Looking good was the easiest step in Nat's approach to winning. He had grown into a fine-looking young man. Women described him as tall, dark, and handsome. He had charisma and a smile that caused men and women alike to want to be around him. As a young boy, he had been very shy, but when he found the thing he was good at, he developed a level of confidence that, coming from anyone else, might have been interpreted as arrogance. When he walked into a bowling alley, it was as if a celebrity had entered. Everyone loved him and respected the focus, discipline, and talent he had for the game. It was during what was to be an ordinary tournament that life for Nat and his team members changed.

Nat prepared for the tournament according to his normal routine. He neatly packed one small suitcase, bringing with him his "dress to win" attire: a pair of tailor-made dark green trousers; a lighter green starched short-sleeved shirt; a new pair of dark green socks; and of course his size fifteen dark green bowling shoes. Green had always been his favorite color, and Nat believed that wearing it added to his confidence. So as he began earning money from his winnings, he had his pants and shirts custom made in various shades of green. His bowling shoes were special ordered not just because of the size, but also because Nat was meticulous about the color.

The flight to Cincinnati arrived on schedule, with plenty of time for Nat to join his teammates at the hotel. The team had decided to drive from Detroit the night before, but Nat taught bowling classes to a group of kids from his neighborhood on Thursdays after school, so he flew. He would join the team on Friday evening for a big tournament Saturday morning.

The cab driver who picked him up at the airport was a talkative fellow. "What are you in town for?"

"A bowling tournament," Nat replied.

"Oh yeah? You ever win?"

"Yep."

"You have like . . . trophies and stuff?"

"Yep."

"I bet you're the best on your team."

"I'm the anchorman."

"Wow! The anchorman has the power to win or lose the game. I knew when you got in my cab that you were successful at something. You have a *success look* about you. How long you in town for?"

"Just the weekend."

"Do you need anything while you're in town?"

"No, I'm good. Uh . . . I don't mean to be rude or anything, but I'm not up for much conversation right now."

"Oh, hey, man, I'm sorry. I do tend to go on. I mean no disrespect. It's just nice to see a young man doing well. Okay, I'll shut up, but I just want you to know that if you need anything while you're in town, I can get it for you. Anything at all!"

Nat glanced at the cab driver but did not respond.

The driver managed to be silent for about ten minutes.

"We're almost there. In no time, I'll have you at your hotel safe and sound and ready to win that tournament."

"Great," Nat said.

"Can I just ask you one question? I'm just curious about what it takes to be a successful man like yourself. Do you have a code, a philosophy, or something? Something that drives you to win?"

"When I look good, practice my behind off, and make sure I have a positive attitude when I walk on the lane, winning is inevitable. That's my philosophy."

"Wow. That's great. I can see that you look good and carry yourself well, but how much do you practice?"

"Long hours. Every day."

"No wonder you're the anchorman. And what do you do to have a positive attitude when you step on the lane?"

"Well, I try not to talk too much before a tournament. I don't fill my mind with a lot of idle chatter."

"I'm sorry, man. I started talking again. I'm just always curious about successful people, what makes you all tick. I've got a young son, and I like to share with him other people's advice about what it takes to be successful since all I've got going are a few hustles that bring in a little money here and there."

Nat cleared his throat.

"There I go again. Sorry, man. Anyway, if you need anything while you're in town, I can get it. I know you need to feel good before your game."

"What are you talking about?" Nat asked.

"I can get you whatever you want. In fact, I've got a little somethin' with me now."

"Hey, I don't do drugs. That's for losers. I don't drink, I don't smoke, and I don't do drugs. I've seen what that stuff does to people and their families. Just get me to my hotel."

"Hey, I don't blame you; that stuff is dangerous. You sound like you've had some personal experience."

"I've never done drugs, and I never will. I'm good at what I do because I work hard. There's no shortcut to winning. That's a loser's mentality. You do the right things; you get the right results. That's it!"

"Okay, didn't mean to get you all upset," the driver said as he pulled the cab over to the curb. "We're here. I got you to your hotel safe and sound, just like I said I would."

Nat got out, reached into his pants pocket, and pulled out a roll of money. He peeled off a twenty-dollar bill to cover the fare, and then he handed it and a ten-dollar bill to the driver. "Keep the change. And do your son a favor—stay away from drugs and drinking," Nat scolded the driver. "That stuff can ruin your life, and his."

"Successful, a good tipper, and the giver of good advice. Man, you've got it all together," said the cab driver, letting out a sarcastic laugh. "I see why you're so successful. You're a strictly by-the-book kinda guy. Boring . . . but I guess it works for you."

"I play to win. That's all," Nat responded. He grabbed his bowling ball and small carry-on luggage from the driver.

"I'd wish you good luck on your tournament, but you probably don't need it." The driver let out another taunting laugh, got back into his cab, and sped off.

Nat's teammates were waiting in the hotel lobby. As soon as Nat checked in, they were all anxious to get to the bowling alley for a few hours of practice. Nat noticed immediately that Frank had been drinking, and he did not acknowledge him as he did the other two players.

When they arrived at the bowling alley, all lanes were occupied, so the team decided to wait in the bar for an available lane.

"Bartender, set us up with four beers," Frank said.

"Make that three," Nat said.

"Oh yeah, I forgot you don't like to drink before you bowl. But we're just practicing," Frank said.

"That's the difference between me and you," Nat snapped at Frank. "You're here to practice; I'm here to win a tournament this weekend."

"Okay, you two, let's have a peaceful night," Reggie said. "We're all on the same team, and we're all here to win." Looking at Frank, he added, "One beer, all right?"

"It's not like I have a drinking problem or anything. So I like to have a few beers when we bowl. What's wrong with that?" Frank asked as he turned toward Nat.

"Look, I don't want to argue with you tonight, but just so you know, when you have too much to drink, you get sloppy," Nat said.

"Well, you're the anchorman. It's your job to hold up the back end, bring us to the win no matter what we leave you to work with," Frank countered.

"That's the problem. When you're drinking, you don't leave me anything to work with. That's why we lost in Dayton two weeks ago—and in Lansing before that."

"You want me off the team, don't you?" Frank asked, anger building in his tone. "Go ahead . . . admit it."

"As a matter of fact, I do," Nat replied. "I just don't think you play to win anymore. You have a job at the factory. But bowling is how I make my living, so yeah, I want you off the team."

"Okay, guys, let's all just calm down," Reggie said. "We can talk about this some other time. Let's win this cash, go back to Detroit, and settle all this. We need to stay focused this weekend."

"This isn't over," Frank said. He grabbed his beer from the counter and went to sit alone at one of the tables in the bar.

"Why did you have to bring that up now?" Reggie asked Nat.

"Because one beer will be five before the night is over, and I want us to get a good practice in tonight. I need to win this tournament. I can use the money."

"Who are you kidding?" Reggie countered. "It's not about the money. You're doing better than any of us are. You love *the win*."

"Okay, I do," Nat admitted. "I love to win. So what? What I also love is to play by the rules with teammates who take the game seriously."

"We all want the same thing, but look, man, getting Frank all upset won't help," Reggie said. "We'll talk to him next week. I think he's ready to quit the team anyway. Something's bothering him—can't you tell?"

"Yeah, what's bothering him is that he drinks too much," Nat said.

"You must've noticed that he's not his old self. I'm telling you—something's going on with Frank. He respects you. Talk to him."

"There's nothing to talk about," Nat said. "Either he stops drinking, or he's off the team. Anyway, Mike told me he was going to drive up this weekend to watch us. He's ready to step in as soon as we get Frank off the team."

Jack, the fourth member of the team, finally spoke up. "Mike's coming this weekend?"

"You talked to him?" Reggie asked.

"Yep," Nat said.

"I thought we would all talk to him together," Reggie said.

"The opportunity came up, so I took it," Nat said. "He's on board, and he's ready."

Finally, a lane became available, and the team practiced for three hours. Nat seemed more serious than usual. He usually laughed and joked a lot with the guys, but Frank continued to drink as they practiced, and with each drink, Nat grew more and more disgusted with him. After practice, Nat left the bowling alley without saying a word to any of his teammates, going back to the hotel alone.

The next morning, the team met for breakfast at six thirty, their regular custom before a tournament. Frank started the day with lots of talk about their need to win. The previous three tournaments had been two total disasters and one third-place trophy. Frank had played well below his average for the last nine months, but the last three tournaments were his worst.

Nat was quiet. He'd had a good night's sleep and had it in his mind to win. He had gone over his three-step philosophy and felt ready in spite of Frank's excessive talking.

The tournament started on time and the team played extremely well in the first game. But as the day progressed, Frank did what he had done at most of their recent games—he ordered a drink.

"Hey, come on, let the drinking go until we finish here," Reggie said. "We're on a roll. If Nat sees you drinking, you know a big argument will start, and that will be it for our winning streak."

"You think I can't handle one drink?" Frank's voice began to escalate. "What's wrong with you guys? Bowling used to be fun, but now it's like we're in the army or something. There's a rule for everything, even drinking. Back in the day, we bowled, we won, we had a good time."

Jack overhead the conversation and walked over to Frank and Reggie. "Frank, don't drink. We really need the win. I'll personally pick up the tab for our first round, but after we're done, all right?"

"Oh, I see. You guys want me off the team too. You're all in this together. It's not about my drinking; you want me off." Frank's voice got even louder. "You think I don't know what's going on? You think I'm stupid? Well, fellas, you don't know who you're dealing with. Frank Johnson doesn't have to take this crap. I don't need to bowl for a living. I bowl so I can—"

"Keep your voice down," Jack said. "You'll get us kicked out."

At that moment, Frank looked at the front door, where he saw Nat talking to Mike, a young bowler who was gaining a reputation as a rising star. "What's he doing here?" Frank asked. "Is that the plan? You guys want me out so you can put Mike in, is that it? Somebody tell me. Is that the plan?"

"Frank, you just don't take the game seriously anymore," Reggie said.

"Oh, you want serious?" Frank stepped over to the bench where they had been sitting, grabbed his jacket, reached into the inside pocket, and pulled out a gun. "Now talk to me about serious. Does this look like I'm serious?"

As screams rang through the bowling alley, Nat quickly joined his team members. "Frank, you don't want to do this. We can work all this out. Put the gun down. Let's step outside and talk like we used to. Come on. We can work this out without the gun."

Frank looked crazed and confused. He waved the gun as though it were a toy. "I just wanted to hang out with you guys. You've been the brothers I never had, and now you want me off the team. Six years we've been together and you treat me like this? This team is all I have. Do you hear me, Nat? How could you do this to me? You were just a kid when I met you. I looked after you when Eli left—like we were flesh and blood. Back in the day, you cared about people. Now all you care about is winning. And you're kicking me off the team? Do you know how much that hurts? Do any of you know how much this hurts?" The sound of the gunshot filled the entire bowling alley.

The guys sat in the waiting room for hours. A doctor came out at one point and said they were doing everything they could. Several hours went by before the doctor came out again. He stood for a moment before saying, "I'm sorry. He's gone."

After the funeral, the guys didn't talk for two weeks. None of them went to the bowling alley for fear someone would want to talk about what had happened in Cincinnati. As much as they all loved the game, the memory of that day kept them away from what once held them together.

Early one morning they each received a call from an attorney, telling them to appear in his office concerning a legal matter. They arrived in suspense.

"Well, gentlemen, first let me say I'm sorry for your loss. It appears you've lost a good friend. A man who, according to what he says in his last will and testament, loved you all like brothers. Frank came to me about a year ago and had me draw up his will. I don't know if you know about his financial affairs, but he came into quite a bit of money when his wife, Clare, died ten years ago. He won a wrongful death suit that made him a wealthy man. He wanted to maintain a normal life, so he kept his job at the factory and spent very little of the money. He invested it, and it's now a rather substantial amount. Without living relatives, he left it all to you."

"Wait just a minute. Are you saying that Frank had big money . . . and that he left it to the three of us?"

"You're Reggie, right?" the attorney asked.

"Yes."

"Frank said you'd be the first to speak up. Well, Reggie, you summed it up correctly. Frank left close to five million dollars to the three of you. He even left you all the money in his pension fund from his job at the factory. With the exception of the life insurance policy, you all should receive everything he had, including personal possessions and his house, which is paid for free and clear."

"The life insurance policy? I thought you said he had no living relatives," Reggie said.

"That's right. But since it was a suicide, the insurance company is denying the claim. I tried to make a case for it since Frank was dying anyway, but they haven't been very cooperative. I can still work on them a little more, once I get Frank's medical records."

Nat spoke up. "What do you mean, 'Frank was dying anyway'?"

"You didn't know?" the attorney asked.

The three looked at each other, shaking their heads.

The attorney said, "I'm sorry. I thought since you all were so close that he had told you."

"I feel sick," Jack said.

"Me too," Reggie said.

"Surely you knew he was ill." The attorney looked at each of the men. "The weight loss and change in his disposition was noticeable."

"He started drinking heavily about a year ago," Nat said. "That was it. He knew he was going to die." Nat held his head down. "He knew he was dying."

"Gentlemen, let me give you some time to take all this in. My secretary will call you in a few days and set up another appointment for the reading of the will. You have some big decisions to make. Nat, you must have been closest to him. He wanted you to be the executor of the estate. He said something to the effect that you would always do the right thing and make sure all the rules were followed."

It took three years before the Frank Johnson Community Center was completed. It was a state-of-the-art recreational facility with an indoor swimming pool, outdoor basketball and tennis courts, computer room, game room, and of course a few lanes for bowling. The center was open to the entire community and located just a few blocks from where Frank had lived for over thirty years. The remaining team members became closer than they were before, though none had picked up a bowling ball since that day in Cincinnati. They spent all their time making sure Frank's memory would be honored. They were especially proud of the fact there was something at the center for all ages, the kind of place the "old Frank," who took Nat under his wing as a young boy, would have liked.

In the lobby, a beautiful display case held the pair of bowling shoes Frank had worn on his last day. The inscription: "These belonged to Frank Johnson, a brave man who loved the game but cared for his teammates, whom he called his brothers, even more."

Sole Thoughts

> *And also if anyone competes in athletics,*
> *he is not crowned unless he competes according to the rules.*
> 2 TIMOTHY 2:5

Bowling shoes represent the opportunity we have before us whenever we accept the invitation to engage in competition. However, when we strap on the "shoes of competition," it is all too easy for the rules of engagement to become overshadowed by the enticement of victory. The very idea of winning is seductive. It flirts with our innermost desires for love, recognition, and acceptance. For some of us, the allure of holding the prize can be mesmerizing to the point of obsession. Those who are weak to the temptations of winning may try to win by any means necessary; the inner voice of solid reasoning and good judgment is then led astray and held hostage in silent arraignment. When enthusiasm goes unchecked, we may do and say things that are out of character. Zeal, the pure energy force that beckons us to leap without looking lurks in the mind ready at the mere possibility of a win. When zeal guides our actions unaccompanied by wisdom and love, integrity wanes and we seek opportunities to manipulate the outcome until all sense of fair play and honesty have been abandoned. When zeal acts as raw enthusiasm, we're willing to get to the finish line even if it means trampling over our opponents, teammates, and in some cases, our own friends. This is competition at its worst.

Obsessing about winning hijacks our thought process and clouds our view. It alters our normal emotional responses and diminishes our mental ability to perform at our highest potential. Winning is not its own reward, for each person has his or her own individual motive for competing. Behind those motives can be a range of thoughts, feelings, and emotions that may be susceptible to corrupt methods of attaining the title of "winner." For some, their desire is to possess the title. Some may have something to prove to self or others. Still others may seek the things that winning promises, such as money, accolades, recognition, or gifts. No matter the motives, no one wants to be considered the opposite of a winner, which is commonly believed to mean loser.

Since competition is part of our current cultural and social structure, it is an act of personal responsibility to learn how to compete in honorable ways that allow us to express our best self. Competition can be an opportunity to stretch ourselves into the next level of proficiency. It offers a chance to display our talents for others to enjoy, to express what we've learned, and to test our skills outside our own training laboratory. In honorable competition, we have the opportunity to acknowledge and celebrate the work of others, and perhaps find our own creativity stimulated with new ideas.

Rules matter, whether we're competing for a job promotion, a lead role in the school play, or first place in a sporting event. Our challenge is to learn to participate according to the stated guidelines as well as the principles of *honorable* competition that are all too often not stated. The stated guidelines speak to the outer experience, the actions we take to attain the prize. The unspoken principles relate to the inner preparation that shapes ethics, respect and honesty. The inner work involves tugging the human heart away from the obsession to win at all costs, moving it toward justice, fairness, and compassion. In this way, we discover that there is a nonphysical path to triumph, where we can never lose if we give the best of our attitude, and character, as well as our skills and talents. And while zeal can be used to help us move enthusiastically toward our goal, it needs the balance of wisdom and love to assure that we honor, respect, and care about people around us—those we compete with and those we compete against.

No matter what the outer prize, the inner prize will be with us long after the competition is over and the trophy is covered with dust. If we strive to uphold integrity and honesty as we cultivate our craft, we will build true champion status into the very fabric of our character, and that's when losing will not be an option. That's when competition works, and everybody wins.

Extraordinary Step to Empower Your Sole's Journey

Use your zeal to give your inner and outer best in whatever you do. Claim the attitude that you are already a winner, for you are a child of God.

If the Shoe Fits . . .

- Have you ever been in a situation where your zeal to win became an obsession? If so, describe what you experienced.
- Describe a competitive situation where you did not come in first place. How did you feel?
- Choose a pair of shoes from your closet and write an inscription for them that reflects a truth about you. Example: "These are the shoes of _____, who _____."
- In the story, how could the situation with Frank have been handled differently?
- What ways can you think of to help teach children the principles of honorable competition?
- What would be an Extraordinary Step toward achieving some goal in your life if you applied the enthusiasm of *zeal*, balanced with wisdom and love?

12

Royal Sandals

"G RANDPA, TELL US YOUR STORY," six-year-old David requested. "Please, please, Grandpa," his twin brother, Benjamin, pleaded. "We love when you tell us your story."

"Okay, boys," their father said. "Your grandfather is probably tired. We've all had a long—"

"It's okay, son," the old man said. "I love to tell my story. It's always a chance for me to recall the day my life was changed forever." He cushioned himself in the large plaid easy chair near the front window. He laid his cane on the floor and signaled with his right hand to the two boys. "Come sit by your old grandpa."

"All right," the father said to his sons. "But after Grandpa's story, it's off to bed."

The boys moved close to the old man and sat on the floor at his feet. They had found an immediate love for hearing their grandfather tell stories, but they especially liked to hear *his* story. They had heard it a few times since the old man moved in with the family three months earlier, but each time their enthusiasm was as if they had never heard it before.

"My father was one of the wealthiest men in the town where we lived," the old man began. "As wealthy as he was in possessions, he was still wealthier in wisdom and kindness." The old man paused for a moment to look directly at the twin boys, whose eyes where fixed on him. "Your great-grandfather was the wisest, most loving man I've ever known."

"How old were you when you ran away from home?" David asked.

The old man smiled. "I didn't exactly run away, but I did leave home. I was sixteen when I went to my father and asked him to give me the money he'd always said would be mine and my brother's someday."

"How much money did he give you, Grandpa?" Benjamin asked.

"You always ask the same question," David said to his brother.

"It was a lot," said the old man. "It was more than any young man should have had in his possession at such an unwise age."

"So what happened when he gave you the money?" David asked.

"Boys, your grandpa wasn't very smart in those days. I traveled from town to town, spending the inheritance my father had given me. I spent it on everything imaginable."

In a concerned tone, David said, "You had to eat—"

"He's not talking about food," Benjamin interrupted. "He spent the money on other stuff."

"You're both right. I did have to eat, and I ate extremely well. I dined at the finest restaurants and drank the most expensive wines I could find. I even picked up the tab for many other people to eat really well, and many of them I didn't even know. And yes," the old man said to Benjamin, "I spent my inheritance on a lot of other stuff too, things a young man should not have to buy. I spent money on things I didn't need, things no one should ever have a need for. And then . . . I woke up one day and two people I thought were my friends had stolen what was left of my inheritance. The money from my father was all gone."

"Is that when you were sad?" David asked.

"It was a tough time, David." The old man paused and shook his head. "But it got worse before it got better."

"Were you lonely for your mom and dad?" David persisted.

"I was. I missed my parents in a way that I never had before."

"And what about your brother, Grandpa?" Benjamin asked. "Did you miss him too?"

"Well, my brother is another story." The old man thought for a moment and then said, "Your granduncle Jesse and I were not as close as you two are, at least not until much later on in our lives, so I didn't miss him as much then as I do now. Back then, I just missed being home."

"So what did you do?" Benjamin asked.

"Well, I was ashamed of how I had squandered my entire inheritance. The people I thought were my friends . . . well, it turned out they were not my friends at all."

"Is *that* when you were sad?" David repeated.

"Yeah, I was." The old man smiled to himself. "There I was, a young man—a boy, really—in a strange town, a long way from home, no money, no friends, and no place to stay."

"Is that when you had to sleep with the pigs?" Benjamin asked.

"I'm not proud of it, but yes, I found myself with no place to lay my head, so I slept with the pigs." The old man paused and the boys were mysteriously silent for a few moments. When he continued, the man's voice was soft, as if he were no longer talking to his grandsons but thinking aloud. "Even though I was at my lowest point, things changed when I could finally see what I had not been able to see before."

"What's that, Grandpa?" Benjamin asked.

His voice seemed to startle the old man, and in an instant, his attention was back to the twins, who hung on his every word.

"In a rare moment of clarity, which I've only had maybe three or four times in my entire life, I heard a voice, like a whispering in my ear: 'Go home. Go back to your father.' I fell asleep with those words being whispered to me; it seemed to go on the whole night. When I woke up the next morning, I just knew. I was so sure of what to do that I said it aloud even though no one was with me but the pigs that were sleeping by my side. I'll never forget the words that came from my mouth—'I will arise and go to my father.'"

"Were you still sad?" David asked.

The old man laughed a little at David's persistence and patted his grandson on the head. "Actually, David, I was happier than I had been in a long time. I knew exactly what I was going to do. I just didn't know what I would say to my father, and that's what concerned me." The old man paused and looked off toward the window.

"Are you okay?" David asked.

"He's all right," Benjamin assured his brother. "He always slows down when he gets to this part."

The old man's son came in from the next room, where he had been listening the whole time. "Dad, do you want to stop now?" He placed his hand on his father's shoulder. "It's okay. You can finish the story another time."

"No, no, I'm fine. I was just remembering the moment I walked up the roadway to my father's house. When I saw him, my eyes filled with tears. I was prepared to fall at his feet and beg his forgiveness, beg him to let me be one of his servants if necessary. I was prepared to beg my father to let me be his son again."

"Beg his forgiveness for what, Grandpa? Running away from home?" David asked.

"He told you he didn't run away. He left home because he wanted the money," Benjamin said.

The old man forced a faint smile on his face. "I wanted my father to forgive me for leaving home the way I did, for throwing away my portion of the inheritance that he had worked hard to earn for my brother and me, for not staying in touch when I left, for disgracing our family name, for returning home in rags—without even a pair of shoes on my feet. It was quite a long list."

The old man's son, who had never heard the story before, spoke up. "Go on, Dad. Then what happened?"

"The moment my father realized it was me, his youngest son, walking up the road, he ran toward me. When he was still a great distance from me, he opened his arms wide and continued running. I wasn't expecting him to do that. My father running toward me with open arms was a sight I've never forgotten. Even now I can see him running toward me." The old man closed his eyes for a moment before he continued. "My father was up in years, and it took great energy for him to run such a distance. With tears streaming down his face, he grabbed me and hugged me for a long time. He held me so tightly that I could feel his heart pounding in his chest. It was a moment I never wanted to end. I knew then that I never wanted to be separated from him again." The old man stopped his story, obviously trying to fight back tears. He threw his head back and looked up at the ceiling.

"Grandpa, it's okay." David stood up and patted his grandfather's hand. "You're here with us now. You don't have to be sad anymore. You can stay with us as long as you want to."

Using his whole hand to wipe the tears from his face, the old man said, "Sometimes in their old age, men cry tears for the actions of their youth."

"Dad, we can finish the story tomorrow," the boys' father said. "Remember what the doctor said about your heart. Besides, the boys have heard the story before."

"Please, Dad, let Grandpa finish. Please, please," David pleaded.

"I'd like to finish my story," the old man said. "And yes, the boys have heard it several times, but you have not. And who knows how long I'll be around to tell it?"

"All right," the boys' father said. "But we should wrap it up." He looked at his sons. "You two have school tomorrow."

"Go ahead, Grandpa. What happened after your dad hugged you for a long time?" David asked.

"He kissed me. First on the right cheek, then on the left, and again on the right, and again on the left. Then he held me by my arms and looked at me. 'You're so skinny. You haven't been eating,' he said. He looked at my worn clothing and then at my bare feet. He shook his head. 'My son, my son,' he said in disbelief, 'you have walked a long, rocky road to get here. Your journey has brought you home without shoes on your feet.' By this time, my mother came out to greet me. She was a soft-spoken woman, but when she saw me, she lifted her voice. 'My boy, my dear sweet boy is home. God in heaven has answered my prayer. My boy is home.' She grabbed me and held me to her bosom the way I imagine she had when I was a baby. She held me in silence for a long time."

"Where was your brother?" David asked.

"Yeah. Did Granduncle Jesse come to meet you?" Benjamin asked.

"He was out in the field with some of the workers, so he didn't know I had returned home. It was much later that evening before I saw my brother—and several days later before he and I talked. He was not as glad to see me as our parents were."

"When did your dad give you the party?" Benjamin asked.

"My father was so happy I was home that he told his servants to prepare me for a king's welcome. 'Bring out the best robe,' he told his servants, 'and put it on him, and put a ring on his hand and sandals on his feet' (Luke 15:22). When I tried to tell my father all that I had done, he wouldn't hear of it. I was home, and that's all that seemed to matter to him. My father went to his grave without once asking me about the inheritance. It was obvious—I had left home with a healthy physique, dressed in fine clothes, expensive shoes, and bags and bags of money. When I returned home, I was frail, dressed in rags, barefoot, no bag over my shoulder, and my eyes filled with tears and shame. He didn't need the details."

"But what about the party, Grandpa? Tell us about the party," Benjamin continued to probe.

"Oh, what a party it was. Nearly everyone from town came. My father was well respected, and when word got around that his son had returned home, people came to join in the celebration. My father spared no expense. There was music, dancing, food, and wine—lots of wine."

"Is that when they killed the calf?" David asked.

"That's right. I forgot you like that piece of trivia in my story." The old man smiled, his mood uplifted again. "Yes, my father told his servants to kill the fattest calf they could find. It was the best meal I'd had in months. There was so much food that there were leftovers for nearly a week. The night ended with my father giving a big toast in my honor. 'Everyone lift your glasses,' he said. 'Drink up. Drink to my son who was lost and now is found. Drink for my son who has come home.'" The old man looked out the window for a moment and then added, "I never left my father's house again. That is, not until I moved here to be with you boys three months ago. When I married your grandmother, God rest her soul, and told her my story, she insisted that we live with my parents. My father and my mother were glad to have us at the house. Leaving that old house was one of the hardest things I've ever had to do."

"Don't you like being here with us?" David asked.

"Of course I do." The old man patted both boys on their heads. "I just don't like being a burden to your mom and dad, and I don't want you boys to worry about me."

"Dad," the boys' father said, "you're not a burden at all. We just don't want . . . well . . . with Mom gone and your health the way it is, we don't want you to be alone. Besides, the boys love having more time with you."

The boys stood up, threw their arms around their grandfather's neck, and said in unison, "I love you, Grandpa."

"Okay, boys, that's enough for one night. You've tired your grandpa. Let's get you both ready for bed."

"Can Grandpa come and tuck us in?" David asked his father.

"Do you feel up to it, Dad?" the boys' father asked.

"I'd like nothing more than to kiss my grandsons good night. I'll be there in a few minutes."

Moments later, as the boys lay in their beds, the old man limped into their room without his cane. He sat in the chair between their twin beds. He seemed out of breath and tired. His son stood in the doorway.

"Good night, my dear grandsons. I love you both so much, more than mere words can say. I hope you will remember that always."

"Grandpa, there's something you never told us about your story," Benjamin said.

"What's that?"

"Whatever happened to the robe, the ring, and the sandals your father gave you?"

"I carry them with me wherever I go."

"What do you mean?" David asked.

"Well, I gave them to your granduncle Jesse on the day our father died. But all that they represent is engrained in my spirit. The meaning behind those precious gifts is locked in my heart."

"Why did you give your brother the gifts your father gave you?" Benjamin asked.

"Well . . . my brother never had the picture in his head of our father running toward him with open arms and tears in his eyes. He never recognized our father's unconditional love."

"Didn't your dad love both of you, like our Dad loves both of us?" David asked.

"Yes. But we grew up thinking that our father's love was in the things he could give us or do for us. We both had lessons to learn and we chose to learn them in different ways. I went away; my brother stayed home. Our father's love was not influenced by whether we stayed or moved out. He loved us without condition. My brother was jealous the day our father gave me the robe, the ring, the sandals, and the big celebration. He didn't understand that as expensive as those gifts were, as grand as the party was, they were no measure of our father's love. On the day Father died, I watched my brother grieve, not just because he missed our father, but because he never understood how much Father loved him. So I gave him all the gifts Father had given me so many years before."

"What did you say to him?" Benjamin asked.

"I told him I felt his pain. I told him what had happened to me when I left home. I told him I went searching for something that I couldn't find in all my travels. All that I had been searching for, I already had in our father's love. I told my brother how ashamed I was to come back home penniless, homeless, friendless, and shoeless. I let him know that I held great remorse in my heart for the way I had left home, but it was from that experience that I was able to learn how much Father really loved me."

"Did that make him feel better?" David asked.

"A little. And for the first time ever, my brother and I talked like friends, like the two of you do. Brothers should always be able to talk to one another."

The boys looked at each other and smiled. "So what did you do next, Grandpa?" Benjamin asked.

"Well, we talked late into the night. He told me some things I did not know about him, and that brought us even closer together. Then, in one of those moments of clarity, as I'd had in the pigpen so many years earlier, I heard a whisper: 'Give him the robe, the ring, and the sandals.' I stood up, went to my room, and pulled a box from the shelf. I returned to find my brother sobbing like a lost child. I felt a deep compassion for him that I had never felt before. I realized that all he ever wanted from our father was the same thing I wanted—his love.

"I pulled the robe from the box. It was deep purple with gold embroidery around the neck, bottom of the sleeves, and around the hem. It was a rich piece of cloth, the kind reserved only for royalty because of its rarity and the cost. I don't know how my father came into possession of it, but it was of the finest quality of that time. I placed the robe on my brother's shoulders and asked him to imagine being held in our father's arms. I told him to think of it as a symbol of being clothed in our father's unconditional love. I told him to remember that no matter what happens, he would always be safe in our father's care and keeping."

The old man felt the eyes of his own son upon him. Still standing at the door listening, the boys' father nodded as if to say, *Continue*.

"I looked in the box and pulled out a gold signet ring. It was a heavy piece of pure gold. The ring had been in our family for generations, and I believe it was made for one of the kings in Egypt long ago. I took my brother's right hand in mine and slowly placed the ring on his finger. As I held his hand, I told him to let the ring be a symbol of his eternal unity and oneness with our father. I said the pure gold represented a promise that he would always abide in prosperity and never lack for anything. I told him his true inheritance was beyond measure, and like the circle of the ring, his inheritance was unlimited and everlasting."

"What about the sandals? When did you give him the sandals?" David asked.

"I walked over to the cabinet where we kept anointing oils and a basin full of water for washing our hands. I placed the oil and basin next to where my brother was seated and knelt before him. I washed his right foot and then kissed it. Then I washed his left foot and kissed it as well. I held his feet in my hands and anointed them with the spikenard oil that my father used for sacred ceremonies. Then I blessed my brother's feet. I prayed he would understand that because of our father's love, no matter where his feet took him, that he would always travel on holy ground. I prayed that as he traveled over the rocky roadways of life, he would not suffer for one moment for the rest of his life. I prayed that the path before him would be a straight path upon which he would run and not be weary, walk and not faint. I prayed that his journey would honor the integrity and truth that our father had modeled for us and put securely in our hearts. I prayed that he would walk through the days of his life realizing that he would never be alone, but that he, our father, and I could never be separated because of the powerful bond of love we share."

"Then I asked him if he would wear the sandals our father had given us as though he were royalty and deserving of the best life has to offer. He nodded. I pulled them from the box and carefully put them on his feet. From that day forward, my brother referred to every pair of sandals he put on his feet as his royal sandals."

"That's quite a story, Dad," the boys' father said. "I had no idea."

"I know, son. The lessons we learn in life come to us when we're ready."

"So whatever happened to Granduncle Jesse?" David asked.

"My brother was happier after that day. We grew closer over the years. When he married his beloved wife, Grace, they moved a few towns over, but we kept in touch. He and Grace had twelve children, and my brother was a prosperous and well-respected man for the remainder of his days. He lived a long life and died peacefully in his sleep two years ago. I like to think he's with our father now. I even believe our father ran to meet him with open arms, like he did with me so long ago."

"You mean like when you came back from running away from home?" David asked.

"How many times does he have to tell you that he didn't run away?" Benjamin scolded his brother. "He left home because he wanted the money. Grandpa, tell us what happened to the robe, the ring, and the sandals."

The old man smiled at the interaction between his grandsons before continuing. "Well, the robe was lost in a fire at my brother's house several years before he died. He gave the ring to his oldest son, who proudly wears it to this day. But on the day my brother died, we found that he'd left the sandals for me in a gift-wrapped box near the door of his bedroom. I always thought that was his way of telling me he loved me. I don't know to this day how long the box had been wrapped or how long it had been sitting at his door."

"Do you miss him?" David asked.

"Yes. We wasted so many years being at odds with each other—too many. Yes, David, I miss my brother terribly."

The next day, when the two boys walked in the house after school, they immediately noticed that their grandfather's sandals were not positioned next to the front door as they had been every day for the past three months. They walked into the old man's bedroom, where they found their father sitting on the bed with his head bowed.

"He's gone, boys. Your grandfather wasn't feeling well this morning, so your mother and I took him to the doctor. He died this afternoon." Expecting a sad response to the news, their father said, "Come sit with me. It's okay to feel sad when someone dies."

"No, Dad," David said. "Grandpa would not be sad, so we shouldn't be sad." Just then, David noticed a box near the door. "Look, Grandpa left a box by the door."

Benjamin handed the box to his father. "Open it, Dad. Grandpa left it for you."

The boys' father opened the box slowly. Inside was a pair of sandals that looked barely worn. As he took them from the box, he realized they were heavy. There were jewels and precious stones around the straps, twelve in all. He touched each of the stones one at a time: the ruby, emerald, sapphire, lapis, beryl, topaz, agate, jade, jasper, carnelian, turquoise, and amethyst. He rubbed the bases of the sandals, which were thinly lined with pure gold.

"They're beautiful," David said.

"Wow . . . , it's the royal sandals," Benjamin said.

The man broke down and sobbed.

"Don't cry, Daddy," David said as he reached for his father's hand. "Grandpa left you the royal sandals because he wants you to know that he loves you."

Benjamin took his father's other hand and said with a confidence that seemed beyond his years, "Grandpa wouldn't want us to worry about him. He's okay. He's just going to be with his father."

"And his brother," David added.

The three sat in silence for a few moments, until Benjamin's curiosity got the best of him. "Dad?" he asked in a soft voice.

"What, son?"

"Do you think Grandpa's father ran to meet him with open arms—"

"Like Grandpa told us in his story?" David finished.

Their father wiped the tears from his face, using his whole hand. He then pulled both boys to him and held them in a long embrace. "Yes, boys. I think he did."

Sole Thoughts

See what great love the Father has lavished on us,
that we should be called children of God! And that is what we are!
JOHN 3:1 (NIV)

There is a hidden curriculum within the school of life. The lessons we experience on the journey to commencement day present a paradox. On one hand, we engage in a fierce search for meaning and personal fulfillment that may lead us to travel long distances, physically and mentally. This turns out to be a desperate pursuit of happiness and often one of life's most ironic journeys. On the other hand, after having spent our time, money, talents, emotional and material resources, and tremendous effort searching for something, only to realize when we finally find it, we discover we had what we thought we lacked, all along.

If, like the masses, in search for meaning and fulfillment we blindly followed the examples and advice of those, who themselves, may have been mislead, our worldviews will have been compromised with deceptive messages. We may have assigned erroneous labels to our personal journeys—the journey to wealth, where we seek to possess many material things; the journey to find love, sometimes even before we love ourselves; the journey to fame, where we seek recognition and attention from people we don't even know; or the journey to power, that sends us on a chase after what the world defines as success. What we learn on this trek is that no matter what journey we think we're on, even if it was meticulously and skillfully planned, if it lacks the power of real love, divine love, the hope of attracting a blessed, long-term outcome will be frustrated by layers and layers of falsities.

> *If I speak in the tongues of men or of angels, but do not have love, I am only a resounding gong or a clanging cymbal. If I have the gift of prophecy and can fathom all mysteries and all knowledge, and if I have a faith that can move mountains, but do not have love, I am nothing. If I give all I possess to the poor and give over my body to hardship that I may boast, but do not have love, I gain nothing* (1 Cor. 13:1-3 NIV).

The school of life can be tough at various points along the way, mostly because we have developed faulty study habits focusing on subject areas that are secondary. Since the lessons we learn and the tests associated with those lessons show up in the visible realm, we mistakenly think that the homework is outer work. And yes, some of the work must be done in the outer, but only after we have first done the primary or inner work in the invisible realm of ideas and thought. After a few—sometimes many—failed tests, we get a glimpse of the "father with outstretched arms" welcoming us back home to life's primary lesson. The ultimate success in our life studies comes in a revelation that love is the primary lesson, and that the answers have been safely tucked in the crevices of our own hearts the entire time. As the hidden curriculum begins to expand in our awareness, we come to the understanding that the blessings we have been searching for and the inheritance we sought in distant places were not to be found until we made the journey back to unconditional love—God's love. Our transcripts can then begin to reflect a change from our old faulty study habits to resolutions and remedies that, going forward, will help meet all of life's trials.

However, since our views on love come mostly from experience, it is common to hold an erroneous assessment of what love is, and how we might get possession of it. From an observational standpoint, we could even be led to believe that love is a master of disguise, particularly since it rarely looks like what we think it should, and it seldom arises from the things we hope will attract it. Often what we think is love may more accurately be described as an attraction based on physical chemistry, misguided importance placed on material gifts and possessions, or an exchange of emotional deficiencies. If our appeal toward another is held together by these kinds of representations, we may later discover that the attitude, character, and values necessary to sustain a healthy "love" connection are absent. Soon after attractiveness fades, material possessions decrease in quality or quantity, or as emotional deficiencies heal, so disappears the declaration of love that has been built on shifting sands.

Consider people who "looked like the perfect couple." They always seemed happy and in love, until later we discover that behind closed doors, the union was not as harmonious as it appeared. Likewise, perhaps we've heard the three precious words "I love you," but the sentiment did not always last. The current divorce rate may be indicative of this idea. Sometimes those words proved to be true; other times, those saying the words subsequently acted in ways that were not loving at all. Love does indeed appear to be a master of disguise, and can be a bit fickle as well.

We may try to capture the essence of what we think love is by using various measuring devices. For example, the woman who uses the size of the diamond in an engagement ring to decide whether she will say yes to a marriage proposal. Or the man who believes his love is conveyed in the things he can provide for his family, even if it means spending lots of time away from them. And what of the child who thinks his parents' love is demonstrated by allowing him to do, or have whatever he wants? The belief that love can be measured is one of the challenges that may prevent us from recognizing its true essence and grasping how to practice it in our lives. Love's most popular biblical definition may even contradict what we have been conditioned to believe about it, and how we've attempted to live it:

> *Love is patient, love is kind. It does not envy, it does not boast, it is not proud. It does not dishonor others, it is not self-seeking, it is not easily angered, it keeps no record of wrongs. Love does not delight in evil but rejoices with the truth. It always protects, always trusts, always hopes, always perseveres. Love never fails.* (1 Cor. 13:4-8 NIV)

No matter what emotional, material, or mental measuring plan we use in an attempt to gauge the love we give or receive, we will feel something is missing in our lives until we at least glimpse love's deeper essence. The irony is that love is its own antidote, able to heal us from our erroneous beliefs about it. In this revelation, the way of forgiveness, reconciliation, and oneness are possible. It may surprise us to learn that if we attempt to live from the belief that love never fails, we discover that love never fails us. In this awareness, we find that when we discover real love, there is no shortage and more than enough for all to enjoy, and generously share with each other.

> *And now these three remain: faith, hope and love. But the greatest of these is love (1 Cor. 13:13 NIV).*

The love of God is a powerful magnet that pulls us toward itself from our various locations, states of consciousness, and unique circumstances. No matter where our shoes may take us—on rocky roads or smooth paths—at some point, our life lessons bring us full circle, back into the outstretched arms of divine love. The long-anticipated celebration that we have craved since our birth awaits our soul's return home.

At that moment, we are ready to exchange our tired bare feet for the promises of the royal sandals—a state of consciousness that knows we are unconditionally loved, and because of that love, we deserve to travel as royalty over holy ground wherever we go. As the school of life elevates us to higher and higher degrees of understanding, we shall arrive at the realization that we are, have always been, and forever will be—loved!

Extraordinary Step to Empower Your Sole's Journey

Study love, practice sharing it generously and receiving it graciously—until you become a living expression of it.

If the Shoe Fits . . .

- What is your earliest memory in which you sensed you were loved? Describe the experience.
- Have you ever felt unconditional love from someone? Describe the feeling.
- Have you ever loved someone unconditionally? What was/ is it like?
- What is your belief regarding God's love for you?
- In this story, is there a moment that stands out for you? If so, what is it, and why?
- If you had the mental and spiritual awareness of the idea of the royal sandals, would anything be different about your walk through life? What could such a journey look like going forward?
- In your life right now, what would be an Extraordinary Step toward the realization of unconditional *love*—your true inheritance from God?

In Summary

One Possible Reason to Love Shoes

Since your first pair of "Baby Shoes," you have demonstrated the *strength* that has helped you get to where you are today. You've used your *imagination* to see your way through difficult times, occasionally engaging your "Dancing Shoes" to help celebrate some well-earned victories.

Whether you displayed the masculine swagger of "A Man and His Gators," to exercise your personal *power, or* embodied the feminine grace of sexy "Stilettos," to announce the *release* of old fears, you now know how to exude style, grace and poise with ease.

Perhaps you attained the *wisdom* to balance your use of time through not-so-ordinary means—like precious moments spent during a "Shoe Shine," or from some other experience you will never forget. Out of sheer necessity you learned to acknowledge the divine *order* of circumstances; sometimes following in the footprints of others so that later you might leave "Footprints in the Snow" for others to find their way. Your choices along the journey presented you with opportunities to walk in another's shoes, and "In His Shoes," you discovered the value of cultivating an *understanding* heart, a gift that now blesses all your interactions with others.

Some say it's your "Lucky Shoes" that give you a strong *will* to survive and succeed—unlike you, they have not yet discovered the secret behind the appearance of luck. And although you have made a misstep or two along the way, "Bloody Soles" could not trample your love for *life* nor diminish your belief in the goodness of others. Your *faith* has taught you to look for a blessing in every experience for you've discovered that even a "Broken Heel" on your shoe can be part of an answer to a prayer.

So, whether wearing tennis shoes, walking shoes, running shoes, "Bowling Shoes," or no shoes at all, you've learned to balance your enthusiasm with wisdom and love, and now *zeal* serves you well in all that you do. The extraordinary steps you've taken toward your divine destiny and your return to the outstretched arms of God's unconditional *love*, have left you with the tools to make every pair of shoes you wear worthy of being called "Royal Sandals." Not so much for their style and beauty but because of the love poured into every child of God and the blessing of the holy ground beneath every step we take on life's journey.

Conclusion

More than a Fashion Statement

Put on your shoes so that you are ready to spread the
Good News that gives peace.
Ephesians 6:15 (GW)

I believe there is a metaphysical shoe lover in everyone. That "love," however, is felt, experienced, and expressed in different ways and at varying levels of importance. For some, shoes add the exclamation point to a sassy outfit or a dashing ensemble. For the practical, shoes are about functionality. To them, when it snows, they appreciate a good sturdy pair of boots, and on hot summer days, comfort will defeat a pair of stylish sandals every time. However, most of us live somewhere in between and acknowledge that shoes are about going places. When we're excited about where we're going and what we intend to do when we get there (stylish shoes or not), our "soles" are engaged with vigor, excitement, and great anticipation of a grand adventure.

The stories herein have been about forward movement—physically, mentally, emotionally, and spiritually. Shoes have been presented as providing much-needed support for life's experiences as we wander into corridors of change and passageways of opportunities. Some of the routes we took were smooth and allowed for grand celebrations. Others paraded us through many detours, and we may have felt lost for a while, but we made it through. Following inner guidance, we directed our shoes back to the right path, and again we felt the comfort of knowing our steps were sound and secure. The point is that behind every pair of shoes is a story—some are low-key and uneventful; others leave a deep impression on our hearts and minds.

The stories can tell of the pursuit of love and romance, as revealed by the lost slipper in Cinderella's fairytale; or of the hope and perseverance, as in revealed in *The Wizard of Oz*, when Dorothy's bright red shoes transport her back to Kansas with three clicks of her heels. Perhaps we are inspired just witnessing a fifty-five-year-old man lacing up a brand-new pair of sneakers with a fresh commitment to his doctor's orders to lose thirty pounds. Shoes can be a catalyst for compassionate acceptance, as in Grandpa's loving hug after receiving yet another pair of house slippers for the third Christmas in a row. We marvel at the light in a little girl's eyes as she tries on her first pair of ballet shoes, and instantly we feel a resuscitation of our own childhood dreams. The stories can go on and on. As long as there are hopes and dreams, places to go, journeys to travel, and life lessons to be learned, there will be shoes to help us travel to wherever a blessing can be found.

If you've addressed the questions at the end of each chapter, you may have discovered or rediscovered your own stories that introduced you to levels of self-exploration you had not previously considered. Equipped with new personal discoveries, you have an opportunity to use your shoe stories as lessons that will give you greater power to shape and design the life you desire. Going forward, when you aim toward a goal or desire, address a long-held fear, bring closure to an episode, or begin a new path, your shoes will be empowered for the journey. Each step will compel the next and the next, until you are face-to-face with first the possibility and then the reality of fulfillment.

Armed with empowering steps for your journey, decide where you want to go. Your purpose, goals, and dreams will direct you to the type of shoes that will get you there—walking shoes, running shoes, cross-country trainers, stilettos, alligator skin, house slippers, or whatever. With your soles on the path toward your desires, you can take baby steps or giant steps. It doesn't matter which; just keep your shoes in motion.

As you gain momentum, use your traction to put some real mileage on your shoes. Outer motion can often stir up inner strength and awaken your willingness to embrace causes beyond your own. With great vigor, you'll have the prerogative to march boldly or walk softly, spreading love, peace, and happiness wherever you go. As you endeavor to chart the path toward your best life, others will notice your shoes—not just for their style and color, but also for the good works you accomplish while wearing them.

Opportunities to leave honorable footprints for others who might otherwise lose their way will come to you under divine grace. With good intentions in your heart, your steps will be magnetic, and others will be inspired to stand tall and proud in their shoes next to yours. Perhaps you'll walk a mile or two in another's shoes, run a marathon for a worthy cause, or teach a dance class in your community. You might even use your shoes to stand up for some injustice in the world, or maybe you'll just give a pair of shoes to someone who has none. The possibilities for casual shoe lovers are great. The possibilities for metaphysical shoe lovers are endless!

Any morning you put on a pair of carefully selected shoes with the intention of walking through an incredible day for the purpose of living a high-quality life, you'll know for sure that shoes are so much more than a fashion statement. You will have activated your inner power to choose extraordinary steps that hold the potential of safe passage on wondrous journeys to places and experiences beyond your greatest aspirations.

About the Author

Charline E. Manuel is a spiritual leader, inspirational teacher, lecturer, and author. Ordained by Unity School of Christianity in 1995, she has over seventeen years as senior minister in congregational ministry. She has encouraged thousands of people through her Sunday messages, lectures, seminars, workshops, and international mission initiatives. In her creative style of teaching, she presents personal strategies and spiritual principles with a focus on practical approaches that lend themselves to a positive way of life. An advocate of personal empowerment and youth education, she assists others in the transformation of their lives. In addition to *The Metaphysics of Shoes,* she is the author of *Pray Up Your Life* and the *Pray Up Your Life Companion Workbook*.

Websites: www.themetaphysicsofshoes.com or
www.charlineemanuel.com